ADVANCE PRAISE FOR *l*

Bruce breaks the typical mold for financial advisors. He showed me that there is a way to put the client first in any financial plan—not the commissions. This book should be a "how to" guide for all financial advisors.

—Bill Bartman, Founder and CEO of Bartman Enterprises, one of the Forbes 400 richest Americans and twice named National Entrepreneur of the Year

Bruce Helmer's straightforward approach to life and your money sets this book apart. Bruce offers a superb learning tool for financial decision-making, based on the things people are genuinely passionate about!

—David Horsager, MA CSP, author of *The Trust Edge* and international business strategist

I've known Bruce Helmer for 14 years. He has a knack for finding the weaknesses in conventional wisdom and then coming up with a better financial solution. He also has a unique ability to link our money with important people—as well as the goals we have in our lives. He is certainly among the best financial authors in the country.

—John Castino, MBA, former Major League Baseball player

Real Wealth will cause you to rethink your financial life. It provides a new perspective on money as well as tons of useful information. It is a great read and most importantly, it will inspire you!

—Elizabeth Sarquis Fenn, founder and CEO of Global Gaming Initiative

Bruce Helmer is the real deal. His ideas will help you gain confidence in your financial choices and change your life for the better.

**—Walter Bond, former NBA player and
nationally known public speaker**

Bruce is an educator first and foremost through his radio program and his books. He has sought to provide investors with not only a fresh perspective, but also key advice on the importance of both wealth and happiness. Bruce is an entrepreneur who has built a large financial services organization on these important tenets. His books have been passed around to my family members and my closest friends, and every one of them have commented to me that Bruce's perspectives were eye-opening and useful.

Bruce comes from a humble background where trust is the foremost quality one can have in business dealings. Bruce has never wavered from this heritage. This book is no exception—it drives home the key principles by which Bruce has helped thousands of clients over the past twenty-five years. I know that you will enjoy reading *Real Wealth* as much as I did!

**—Jeff Montgomery, Chairman and Chief Executive Officer
of AFAM | Innealta Capital**

Updated edition of *Money and the People You Love*

REAL WEALTH

How to make **Smart Money Choices** for what matters most to **YOU**

BRUCE HELMER

Weekly Radio Host of the "Your Money" Show

ISBN 13: 978-1-59298-569-2

Library of Congress Catalog Number: 2012920903

Printed in the United States of America.

First Printing: 2013

17 16 15 14 13   5 4 3 2 1

Edited by Connie Anderson.
Cover and interior design by James Monroe Design, LLC.

Beaver's Pond Press, Inc.
7108 Ohms Lane
Edina, MN 55439–2129
(952) 829-8818
www.BeaversPondPress.com

BEAVER'S
POND
PRESS

To order, visit www.BeaversPondBooks.com
or call (800) 901-3480. Reseller discounts available.

This book is dedicated to Laura, my loving wife of twenty-five years,
and to Ali and Greg, our beautiful children.
They teach me something new every day.
With everything I do, or don't do, personally and professionally,
I think of them first and foremost.
Family is my most important personal value.
Laura and the kids are my inspiration—without them, I am nothing.

CONTENTS

FOREWORD

Bruce Helmer first published *Money and the People You Love* in 2006. It was good then, and it was important then. This updated edition, now titled *Real Wealth*, is even better, and it is more important now than ever. Congratulations for choosing to read it. You will not be disappointed; you will be encouraged. Enjoy!

Bruce understands it's not about the money. It's about values. It's about your values, not his or mine. Yours. And because the title of this book attracted you to read it, I am going to make the assumption that you know that the real wealth in your life is from the things you value and the people you love.

Money itself doesn't matter. With the extraordinary help of my collaborative writer and colleague, Kathy Jordan, I wrote the book *Financial Intelligence: How to Make Smart, Values-Based Decisions with Your Money and Your Life*. But before that became the title, my working title was *Making Money Matter*. Bruce understands how to make money matter, and how to put it to work for your real wealth. And he's sharing with you his understanding. As I see it, there are three ways money can matter:

1. How one goes about making money can matter. In other words, one can choose to make money make a difference. That is the choice Bruce has made and that is the choice you can make for yourself and the choice you can influence for the people you love.

2. One can make money matter by being responsible with it. Being responsible is about living within one's means. It's about not relying on family or friends or government to make ends meet. It's about not betting that nothing bad will ever happen to our health or to the economy. In short, it's about being accountable for the responsibilities we have taken on for ourselves, for the things we care about, and for the people we love. Bruce understands this and he articulates it well as he writes about financial fundamentals and money management and planning for the certainty of uncertainty.

3. One can also make money matter by using it to help those less fortunate. If it happens that you have taken care of your responsibilities, and if it happens that after doing so you are left with a surplus, then you can choose to use some of your money to make a difference for those who are not as blessed as you are. Bruce understands this also, as he writes about being generous and teaching generosity.

I've known Bruce for a number of years, and before getting to know him personally and professionally I became a fan of his by listening to his popular *Your Money* program on WCCO radio in Minneapolis/St. Paul. Bruce makes his income making a difference. Bruce is himself responsible. And Bruce doesn't just teach generosity, he and his wife Laura live it.

And it all starts with understanding what real wealth is. Real wealth is being able to use your time and money in ways that support the people and things that mean the most to you: family, friends, places, organizations, and causes. Love yourself for making the choice to invest in your real wealth. And please use and share *Real Wealth* with others in your life.

—Doug Lennick
CEO, the Lennick Aberman Group
Author or co-author of five books, including internationally
acclaimed *Moral Intelligence*,
Moral Intelligence 2.0, and *Financial Intelligence*.

INTRODUCTION:
What's Important to You?

We are social beings, and our identities are inextricably linked with others: I am Joe's son, I am Sally's mother, and he is a friend of mine. I grew up in Olivia, Minnesota, population about 2,500. I knew everyone, everyone knew me—and my family history—and I knew theirs. This is why I feel personal connections acutely.

I have learned that almost everyone, from any environment or culture, privately if not publicly, describes themselves by their relationships to other people—those with whom they laugh and cry, work and study, play and worship. We dream with others. We hope with others. We mourn with others. We are nurtured, protected, and defended by grandparents, parents, siblings, spouses, children, and friends, and in turn we nurture, protect, and defend them. Our eyes mist up, our throats tighten, sometimes tears flow just on seeing an image of others—even unknown others—in pain or sorrow.

What's really important in our life? Spending time with our families and people we care about most. I am not a doctor, pastor, or counselor to whom people reveal their souls or their secrets. But I am a financial advisor, so I hear people's hopes and dreams. And with very few exceptions, people talk about the people they love and the relationships they hold most dear. Their future, the life they wish to live, is always full of the people most important to them. They don't talk first about dollars and cents, the Dow Jones average, or bond yields. They talk about a spouse or partner, a best friend, a child, or a parent, organizations they're involved in and causes they believe in. People focus on others when imagining their financial futures; employees, friends, faith communities, and charities all have been the focus of planning efforts with my clients.

My work has taught me a simple truth: Relationships are the single greatest influence on how we use our wealth and that's why I wrote my second book, *Money and the People You Love*. We do not live our financial lives in a vacuum. We live and plan with and for others. The two are inseparable.

Knowing Yourself, Your Values

Yes, relationships are of paramount importance. But perhaps even more important is knowing yourself and your own core values. Sometimes identifying and communicating your values can be difficult, even scary. But when you do it, it really puts things in perspective. When you sit down and think about what matters most to you and why—things like loyalty or honesty or spirituality or family or adventure—and then use those values to make financial decisions, it makes a difference; it truly brings your life and your wealth together. If I help one person or one couple or one family base their financial planning on their values and their relationships, then the effort of the exercise is worth it.

Your financial journey should be based on your personal values and when it is, you'll find yourself making better decisions about your money—for you and the ones you love. You'll find that when you know your values, you won't be motivated by greed or fear. You'll find that when markets are volatile or do the unexpected, it's easy to stick with your plan because you've made financial decisions based on your values. When you think about the five things you can do with your money (spend it; save it; invest it; pay taxes with it; leave a legacy—you'll read about all of these later), your decisions about each of those should be guided by your values. A values-based approach to money gives you a foundation in an ever-changing world and it is especially helpful for those who have difficulties making sound financial decisions.

I find over and over again that when I help people understand what matters, why it matters, and what financial decisions mean to their lives, it creates a common frame of reference. And from there, a financial plan that is driven by clarity about values and the resulting goals comes together. And there is a solid foundation—a rock to cling to—when you (and even the smartest investors do this) stop thinking objectively and instead react emotionally. If all of this sounds complicated, it isn't. Think of it as an X-ray of your soul.

Here's an example based on a real couple I work with:

Dave and Carol shared their top two values: family and education for their three children. But as they made more money and their financial situation improved, they confessed to me their desire for a particular luxury car that would double their monthly car payment from $400 to $800. They wanted to know if they could afford it.

We did a cash-flow analysis and determined that, with their new higher income, they could indeed afford the luxury car at $800 a month. And I told them so. But I also reminded them of their values, the importance to them of education for their children, and their love for their family. So I asked them, "Are you sure you want an extra $400 a month to go to a car payment, or would you prefer to have $400 a month go to funding educational accounts for your three children?" Ten seconds of stunned silence later, they agreed with me and decided to stick with their original $400 per month car payment. And then, within the next month, they started systematically contributing $400 a month to education accounts for their children.

Could they afford the luxury car? The answer was yes, but by using a values-based approach, I could remind them of what they already knew: their children's education was far more important. Fast-forward this story three years. Their income continued to go up, and together we determined they had the economic wherewithal to get that luxury car and still continue to fund educational accounts and retirement plans. They could afford both. And they're still happy, grateful, satisfied clients as of this writing in 2012. The bottom line is not that their financial advisor told them what to do; it's that their values gave them a solid, objective standard by which to make decisions. My job was to remind them what was important to them.

For the record, the top five values that I strive to live by are:

1. Family

2. Meaningful work

3. Integrity

4. Loyalty

5. Health

Wall Street, Main Street, and the Great Recession

Having a values-based approach has taken on even more importance since the 21st Century Great Recession, when the historic solidity of the financial world disappeared. Almost every belief about money has been called into question over the past few years.

The importance of saving? Unemployment at a level and duration not seen since the 1930s consumed the savings of tens of millions of people who used their retirement money, college money, and vacation money to eat and pay the rent. The importance of investing? Money invested in equities in 2001 was still worth the same amount in 2011. Rewards for hard work? The real wages of most workers declined between 2001 and 2011. Belief in the strength and honesty of banks, Wall Street, and insurance companies? Their greed and incompetence caused the financial crisis. Belief that government would protect the economy and the financial system? It didn't. Belief that owning a home is always a good investment? It isn't.

I could go on, but I'm only telling you what you already know. The financial world, and people's beliefs about it, continues to shift as I write. Everyone, from the biggest international banks, to politicians, to ordinary people like you and me, is redefining their beliefs about money, its role in their lives, and their faith in the financial institutions that manage, protect, and grow money. That's why asking, "What's important to me?" to determine your core values is a necessary first step to creating a financial plan. It's the only way to get to a solid foundation for your financial decisions, one that won't shift.

We're living in a new economy that is constantly forming and re-forming around us, with few experts agreeing on the next steps. Greed and stupidity seem to be stronger than our collective memory, stronger even than our new government regulations designed specifically to hold them in check.

Where do you turn? What's still solid in the shifting financial landscape? How do you make a plan that is based on what is most important to you? That's why I've updated this book. When I wrote *Money and the People You Love* in 2006, I didn't answer those questions because no one was asking them. Now everyone is. Welcome to *Real Wealth*.

I encourage you to take this book to heart and use it like a friend as you live your life. I believe you'll be more fulfilled as you focus on whatever is most important to you.

CHAPTER 1

Money and the Love
of Your Life

If you're lucky enough to have a spouse or partner, a soul mate, or the love of your life, you and your partner share many things, including responsibilities and dreams for the future. Another advantage of being a couple is pooled resources. But pooled resources are only an advantage if you avoid the pitfalls that trap the unsuspecting or unprepared: shared obligations, as well as two of you spending.

Understanding and communicating your values about money.

The two of you might jointly work to meet financial goals, but it takes only one of you to torpedo a plan. Financial planning with a partner or spouse takes extra care and forethought to reach agreement on your financial goals and to pursue your dreams. As a financial advisor, I see the symptoms of relationship problems, with financial differences often cited as a primary cause of the 50 percent of marriages that end in divorce.

5

The challenge for couples is the tendency to increase spending beyond what either person would spend on his or her own. If you're married, you know how it works: Your husband craves a glass of wine with dinner, a small thing, so you buy a nice bottle of wine even though it's not important to you. You're already splurging, so you buy a chocolate torte for dessert, a delicacy you daydream about, but one that doesn't matter much to him. You both enjoy your respective treats, but you spent more money than you anticipated on items the other person wanted, and that neither of you would have purchased by yourself. It's a silly example, but it gets to the root of many couples' money problems. You can't negotiate the financial implications of every craving, so you indulge each other. Or maybe she hates the rug that you like, so she talks you into getting a different one. While you're rearranging your living room, you decide it's time to replace the light fixture that has always seemed just wrong for the room. It makes sense to make all the improvements at once. You hadn't budgeted for either item, but both go on the credit card, and you'll pay off the bill next month. But next month something else comes up, and the balance on your credit card grows.

Or your wife really needs to see her mom in Boston. She sounded lonely and upset on the phone, and you haven't visited in almost a year. You didn't budget for the trip, but it's important. Does that mean you cancel the family vacation you planned for later in the summer? Maybe you can squeeze in both.

Before long you're asking each other, "What happened?" What happened is that your financial life is out of control. As in much else in marriage, you and your spouse react to many subtle clues or behaviors you see in each other—or *think* you see. Despite your talk about sticking to a budget, he buys a new golf putter because he couldn't pass up a great deal. Now you think money isn't as tight as he said it is, and you buy the purse you see on sale.

Expenditures can soar even when you work closely together to manage your money. Imagine when couples don't cooperate on spending or, worse, if they spend spitefully. "If you're going golfing in

Arizona with your friends, then I'm going with mine to Los Cabos." Will you tell your friends you can't go golfing with them? Or will you take it to another level? "Will I still drive the old Honda when you get a new Lexus? Let's lease two new cars." Can you afford both? Will you pass on the Lexus you had your heart set on because you can't afford two new cars? Probably not. Even if you don't get two new cars, you might get the Lexus, but then your wife goes to Los Cabos.

It can get worse, much worse. Every person has a spending comfort level that can be exceeded by part of a couple, and often without the partner's recognition or understanding. Throw in the unexpected expenses that come with children and you have a financial mess.

Now let's complicate the challenge even more. Let's assume that one of you accepts most of the responsibility for managing your money. Rarely do I encounter in my practice a couple that divides money management equally, regardless of whether they have equal incomes or one of them earns considerably more than the other. It's often a matter of affinity or interest in financial affairs. In my experience, men are generally more likely to manage a couple's finances, although that is changing, and many more women are now also looking after "future" big-picture money management: savings, investments, retirement accounts. Household spending, while it used to generally be handled by women, is now much more a joint endeavor. Whoever and however you choose to manage the different components of your financial lives is fine. Any system can work for couples as long as both know, and agree on, the goals, status, and progress toward meeting them.

That's one of the advantages of working with a professional financial advisor. Periodic meetings with an advisor—quarterly, semiannually, or yearly—give both partners a chance to agree on the details, direction, and progress of their financial plans.

When one partner manages all the finances, without regularly updating the other, what happens if one makes riskier investments, spends more, gets sick, or dies? Now all of a sudden you may have investment losses, debt, medical bills, or bills associated with a death, and the surviving partner or spouse is left in the dark about finances.

Men usually manage the money, and men usually die first. And consider that women's life expectancy is 80.8 years, compared to age 75.7 for men.

Because life is uncertain, it is important that both people in a relationship be involved in financial planning. At some point, one of them will be left to manage the finances—and alone, he or she will suffer the consequences of poor financial planning. The financial benefit of marriage often disappears because of lack of control over spending and lack of communication about financial planning.

In this section I will discuss the four most important financial planning issues partners face together:

1. Money management;

2. Planning for emergencies;

3. Planning to improve life; and

4. Planning for retirement.

Before we dive into the challenges of managing money with your spouse or partner, here's another challenge that is increasingly common: couples who work together in a family business. If you think marital finances can get complicated, just try adding joint responsibility for business decisions. Joint ownership or management of a business places unique strains on a relationship. If you decide to work together, seek the advice of a good accountant, and perhaps have an informal "board of directors" that can help you make important financial decisions. You will have to plan personal finances with special care because both of your incomes are tied to the same enterprise, which can be tricky, especially in start-up companies where revenues are unpredictable. Establish realistic personal financial plans for each of the areas addressed in this section. Careful personal financial planning is as important as careful business planning, but it can be forgotten amid the day-to-day stresses of running a business.

Money Management

Most couples divide money issues into two categories: 1) periodic or regular expenses, and 2) savings or investments to finance future goals and plans. Usually, one half of the couple is responsible for the first, and one for the second. In previous generations, women have generally been responsible for paying the bills and men generally do the investing. However, this is changing, and the division of labor with regard to finances seems to be much more equal now—and that's a good thing. Successful money management requires that those lines be erased because spending and saving are interdependent. The money comes from the same sources, and the more you spend on one, the less you can spend on the other.

So you should be jointly managing all money in your household, and you should both agree on your financial priorities. It doesn't matter if $100 is mere pocket change to you or if it is your monthly savings. The same principles apply.

Consider the life expectancy and money statistics mentioned earlier. Women *especially* need to be equal partners in long-term financial planning because they will be the ones who live with the success or failure of the financial plan. That's not a morbid thought, but a statistical likelihood. Become a team now, regardless of your age or health. It's time.

- If you are a woman who has deferred to her husband on financial matters, get involved while you can still affect your financial future.

- If you are a man who has made all the long-term financial decisions, bring your wife up to speed. Don't make her learn while she is grieving your death.

Here are the areas in which you and your partner need to coordinate money management to have the best possible financial future:

Budgets

Agree on goals, divide responsibilities, and share information with each other. Find out what a realistic budget is to meet his or her needs. For instance, men often don't realize what their wives spend on lipstick, moisturizer, or hairstyling, let alone on a pair of shoes. A woman might not realize that when her husband says he's going to an NBA game with some buddies, he may have to spend close to $100 for a decent seat.

The key is not just how much you spend, but whether your spending is consistent with your priorities and plans.

Computer software programs, such as Quicken, can make it easier to see how much you are spending on what, and to periodically review how you are doing against your current budgets. Periodic reviews are essential—either together as a couple, or with your financial advisor. Most of all, avoid surprises. If you spend a few extra bucks on a circular saw or a bracelet, share your joy before the credit card bill arrives. Here's a good rule: If you have to hide what you spend, don't spend it. Budget-busting spending on discretionary items snowballs.

Bank Accounts

Maintain separate checking accounts. In both my professional and personal experience, this alleviates stress in a relationship. Regardless of income, partners shouldn't have to be looking over their shoulder every time they write a check. Separate accounts provide some small sense of freedom. Even if one person doesn't earn an income, he or she should have a separate account for day-to-day expenses.

Credit Ratings

As dangerous as credit cards are, using them regularly—and paying off the balance each month—establishes a payment history and credit rating. Some couples may have credit only in the husband's name, which may particularly be the case for older couples. But if there is a divorce or death, the woman is left with no personal credit history of her own, making it more difficult to obtain credit. Each of you needs to establish a good credit history in your own name.

Benefits

If you both work outside the home, be sure to coordinate your job benefits. Most people get excellent help from their employer's human resource department in determining the best way to coordinate benefits. Most couples understand where to get the biggest bang for the benefit buck, with the one exception being life insurance. Employer-sponsored life insurance policies vary greatly, and can be difficult to compare without experience. Don't assume that your life insurance policy through your employer is cheaper than one you could acquire independently. Employer-sponsored plans often group the unhealthy with the healthy, so if you have no health problems, you may find a better life insurance deal on your own. As the economy changes and more people choose self-employment, pay special attention to finding the most cost-efficient health and disability insurance if neither spouse is covered by employee benefits.

Pretax Retirement Plans and Pensions

Look closely at the asset allocation across both of your employer-sponsored or employer-matched plans as part of your annual or semiannual review of your investments.

Too often the two plans have duplication or imbalance in assets. Your asset allocation should include all assets. When you periodically rebalance your portfolio, be sure to look at both of your 401(k)s and/or pension plans as if they were one, to determine appropriate and balanced allocation. If you cannot achieve the asset allocation you desire between your two plans, investigate your options for diversifying your retirement investments beyond pretax plans, especially for any portion of your contributions not matched by your employers.

Taxes

Taxes may be more complex for couples. That could be a good thing. With two incomes, you may have the means to participate in tax-reduction strategies unfamiliar to many people. Or if you are a one-income household as a result of the recession, be sure to investigate further; strategies that reduce taxes are not just for the super-rich.

A great example is a couple in their 50s that came to see me: the husband is retired, but the wife is still employed. The couple has no mortgage or debt, and they can live on the wife's paycheck alone. She also has $92,000 in her savings account. Despite this, the husband started taking early withdrawals from one of his retirement accounts, triggering taxes unnecessarily, because he felt he should still be contributing to the household's income. To demonstrate the inefficiency of this, I listed out all of their sources of income, showing that they had more than enough income to live the lifestyle they had wanted, without the husband taking early withdrawals. This exercise showed the husband how his decision was hurting the couple's finances from a tax perspective.

You should also begin to pay attention to the tax implications of eventual distribution strategies, and the earlier, the better.

- You are probably well aware of taxes on your current income, but most people overlook the potentially significant impact of taxes on the distribution of retirement savings or estates.

- Accumulating assets is the narrow focus of most people, but a plan to distribute those assets requires attention long before retirement comes.

- And don't forget to consider the implications for your distribution strategy, including taxes, or the wife outliving the husband.

Use a Moderator or Mediator

One of the overlooked advantages of working with a professional financial advisor is that he or she can serve as a moderator or mediator for financial discussions. For couples that are having a hard time agreeing on priorities or sticking to plans, an advisor can provide an impartial perspective and a calming voice.

For couples that have never worked together on financial plans before, an advisor can help bridge the gap in knowledge or interest. It's not easy, for example, for a husband of a certain age to bring his wife into discussions of finances when she has participated little, if at all, in the past. Maybe it's frustrating for him to explain some of the financial principles he has learned. Maybe she wants to be included but lacks the knowledge or the confidence to have her say—or to disagree. This description is not sexist in the least. I have seen such relationships many times. This information, as is most in the book, is based on my experiences with real people who are struggling with real issues. I have also seen a shift in recent years where couples now have more similar levels of interest and aptitude for their finances.

A good financial advisor can help couples learn to communicate financial information and evaluate possibilities without the emotional baggage that sometimes accompanies the subject of finances. This is where understanding your values, and what is important to you, can make a huge difference. A financial advisor can initiate talk about the long-ignored elephant in the room and successful financial plans can help remove conflict, spoken or unspoken, in a marriage. Couples with significant assets can have as much money tension in their lives as those scraping to pay their mortgage each month. I've seen many times throughout my career that having a good plan in place to address the issues, whatever they may be, removes a burden from a relationship.

Planning for Emergencies

The Rainy-Day Account

In being prepared for emergencies, the top of the list is to have access to immediate cash to meet your obligations in the short term. Here, I part company with conventional wisdom on the approach to money for emergencies such as sickness, injury, unemployment, or some unforeseen catastrophe.

Many advisors will tell you to keep three months' worth of living expenses in savings or some liquid investment. (By "liquid," I mean money that you could withdraw tomorrow if you needed it.) But since the Great Recession, you have to plan for a far worse case than before. Jobs are less secure, and new ones are harder to find. Lenders, particularly banks, are less forgiving of unpaid debt, and the value of assets that you could draw against, like your house and your retirement savings, have probably gone down. So I recommend maintaining at least six months worth of living expenses in a reserve fund to provide yourself and your family with a bigger cushion.

Perhaps my approach to a rainy-day account is conditioned by the innate conservative nature of the farming heartland where I grew up, and which is part of the economy's foundation in this part of the world. Even if our nation's economy is no longer farm-based, many of our social practices and customs are. Many of us in the Midwest are no more than a generation or two removed from a farm economy. Why do farming areas tend to be conservative? Farmers can't take too many risks, because the price of failure is too high. They get one shot each year at a decent crop, with no fallback position if what you plant doesn't grow or yields too little. Change is measured in years, not weeks.

Protecting the Future: An Introduction to Insurance

The ideal financial plan has contingencies for complications that may arise. What if the primary wage earner loses his or her job? What if someone dies suddenly? What if you become disabled? Ask yourself whether your financial plan will still succeed if an unforeseen emergency strikes your family. Will you still be able to save and invest to have a secure financial future?

Many of the financial plans I review, whether devised by another professional or by an individual, will break down and fail under the worst of circumstances. A plan may look great if life stays rosy, but, unfortunately, life can turn bleak. The ideal plan succeeds in the best and the worst cases. Many advisors and insurance agents focus on the probability of an unforeseen event. I feel it is much more important to focus on the consequences to a family. A great financial plan prepares for the future, but also makes sure that there is a smart place to get money if unforeseen circumstances arise.

Property and Casualty

An important component of worst-case planning is property and casualty insurance, which generally refers to auto and homeowner's insurance. Most Americans have deductibles that are too low, and do not carry enough liability protection.

The lower the insurance deductible (i.e., what you must pay out of pocket before your insurance company will reimburse you), the higher the premium. Let's assume that our auto insurance has a deductible of $250. If we raise the deductible to $500, it saves $50 in premium. If we go only five years without a claim, we can self-insure and be ahead. Even in a worst-case scenario of having an accident and filing a claim every year, it still costs only an extra $250 per year, which has a minimal financial impact on most of us. Deductibles should always be at least $500, if not $1,000.

Let's look at another problem most Americans face, but do not realize it. Consider the following scenario. Your husband is age 45, earns $50,000 per year, and plans to work at least twenty more years. That means he would earn $1,000,000 in those twenty years. But say your husband dies in an auto accident caused by a drunk driver who has only $100,000 of liability coverage on his auto policy, which is common. That person's insurance carrier sends you a check for $100,000. How do you feel? What would you do? Would you consult an attorney and file a lawsuit against the drunken driver? Of course you would, because $100,000 is only a small fraction of the economic value of your deceased spouse.

Now, reverse the situation. What if you make a driving error and someone is seriously hurt or killed. Do you think you are likely to be sued? Of course! Protecting yourself from this potential financial devastation costs roughly the same as carrying the lower deductibles you had. The liability limits should be increased on auto and homeowner insurance, and an umbrella or personal liability policy should be placed over that. Liability coverage is one of the most important, necessary, and affordable things you can ever buy. No matter how much money you make, how much net worth you have, or how great a return you get from your investment portfolio, without proper liability protection, you are only a slip on a banana peel away from financial devastation.

Life changes quickly. Many people commit to investment strategies that they cannot reverse when their life situation changes. It's virtually impossible to anticipate all of our future needs today. Advances in technology, tax law changes, planned obsolescence, and a propensity to consume will complicate and cause changes in our lives. We must have a plan that is adaptable.

The Worst, Worst Case: Life Insurance

What would happen if you died? What would happen if your spouse died? Every couple should ask these questions, whether they have children or not. For most couples, the death of one of them will have a significant financial impact on the other. It could affect their ability to maintain their lifestyle and home. It could affect their ability to save and invest. The answer for most couples is life insurance—on one or both spouses, depending on their circumstances.

In past generations, when many households had only one income earner, protection for the non-earning spouse was more important. In today's two-income households, where the incomes are often roughly equal, the need for insurance for a spouse is less compelling, but for many couples it still exists.

Furthermore, all couples should look closely at life insurance before they have children, because the death benefit is more affordable the younger and healthier you are. Even if you don't have children now, you establish your policy at a lower cost than if you wait.

So let's take a more detailed look at life insurance. Life insurance could also play an important role in your plans for later life as an investment and as an estate-planning tool. Surprised? Most people are.

Life insurance:

1. Is protection for your loved ones. Your spouse (and perhaps children) receives a benefit if you die. It enables others to carry on living without your income.

2. Can provide value as an excellent investment—even if you don't die for a very long time. As I write this, I can imagine a lot of financial gurus leaping to their feet to object: "Life insurance as an investment vehicle? Are you kidding me?" Keep an open mind and read on.

3. Can be a valuable tool in estate planning and charitable giving. Many people buy life insurance as part of their estate planning because beneficiaries usually receive life insurance benefits income tax–free. Life insurance can also be an excellent vehicle for your heirs to pay estate taxes.

Let's begin at the point where most people get stuck when it comes to considering life insurance. They ask, "How much do I need?" Bad start, as they've already turned down the wrong road—and they won't get far.

Do You Need It or Want It?

When people ask me how much life insurance they need, I tell them that life insurance is not a *need* product, it is a *want* product, a love product. If I die before my wife and kids, I want them to have as much money as possible in my absence.

Why do people get hung up on looking at life insurance as a need?

Chances are that you currently have auto and homeowner's insurance. You may also be insured for health care, disability income, and liability risks. But you may never even file a claim on any of these policies. You may never sustain damage to your home, for example, but you cannot afford not to cover that risk.

However, we all die someday. Death is inevitable, but most people aren't willing to face death, so it's hard to convince them that they really do *need* life insurance. If we do consider the possibility, we dismiss it as very remote.

The big question is: Why do we insure assets with less value than our lives against risks that may never occur, and yet we choose not to insure a risk that is certain—death?

Second, when people try to figure out how much life insurance they need, they tend to become immobilized and do nothing.

How do you calculate your life insurance needs? How do you know what your family's needs will be in an indefinite future?

Is homeowner's insurance a *need* product? Let's think about that. Assume you own a home worth $200,000. Does your policy cover the entire $200,000 value? Consider the following scenarios:

- You have $50,000 cash in the bank, which you could access if your house were destroyed, and you needed to rebuild. So would you insure your home for only $150,000?

- You want that $200,000 home, but really only need a home that costs about $125,000. Would you insure your home for only $125,000?

- You have a lake cabin worth $75,000. Nobody needs a lake cabin. So since it's something you only want but don't need, you probably wouldn't insure your cabin at all, right?

Don't these examples sound silly? Obviously, you would insure these assets for what they are worth. That's why we have insurance: to replace things of value. Would it not then follow that you would also insure your life for what it's worth to your family? Most Americans don't. They have been told by nearly everyone that life insurance beyond some minimal level is a waste of money.

The third problem with a focus on need is that most of us are motivated more by what we want than by what we need—especially when that need does not seem urgent. Instead, we spend our money on what we want today.

Even when some people know what's good for them, they don't do it. In 2006, in the first version of this book, I wrote about the case of my clients Jan and Gary, whom I advised to buy variable universal life (VUL) insurance contracts on themselves. They had two very good reasons to be motivated to follow my advice: 1) They had small children and a mortgage, so if either of them died, the survivor would face severe financial hardship, and 2) Jan and Gary were in their early 30s; since the cost would be relatively low, the VULs would be an excellent long-term investment strategy.

They agreed that the life insurance made sense. However, years later, they still haven't taken any action on the policies. Every time I remind them, they tell me they like the idea, but just don't have the cash flow right now, but they soon will. At that point, they'll buy the insurance.

Their reasoning doesn't work for me, however, because I know that both Jan and Gary participate in their company 401(k) plans. I consider the variable universal life (VUL) insurance a better alternative for them at this point than the 401(k)s. Furthermore, they have bought many expensive family toys and taken costly vacations. Obviously, I would consider having this insurance more important than buying a boat or taking a trip.

Why haven't Jan and Gary taken my advice? Likely they see the policies as something they *need*, as opposed to something they really *want*. Sound silly? Would you rather spend your money on medicine or a nice juicy steak? A lawnmower or a snowmobile? Sensible shoes or a new dress?

We are all more motivated by our wants than by our needs.

Even though Jan and Gary feel they ought to have the VULs, the policies have not been a priority, because they don't truly want them. Don't misunderstand my point: I'm not against enjoying life. My challenge as a financial advisor was to demonstrate to Jan and Gary that they really *wanted* the life insurance. They just didn't know it because I had not properly tied the decision to their values. Like Dave and Carol, mentioned previously, Jan and Gary placed great importance on family. They loved their children and each other. I needed to make them realize that the decision to buy life insurance was fundamental to their core values, their goals, who they are, and what's really important to them.

In 2009, after the worst recession in decades and after Jan had a health scare, we met for our annual review meeting. After admitting that the recession and Jan's health scare had changed their perspective and outlook of the future, I asked them if they would be interested in a strategic planning idea that provided a large influx of income tax–free cash if either of them died. I further explained that the same strategy could provide tax-advantaged income in the future. Gary said, "You are talking about life insurance again, aren't you?" I admitted I was. But I asked them if I could focus on what the strategy could do for them, not what it was called.

Jan and Gary finally realized the importance of having life insurance and implemented plans to purchase it that day in 2009.

As long as people treat it as a *need* product, they tend to view life insurance as something they'll get tomorrow, or as a need to meet at a minimum, and then move on.

Those people are missing an important financial opportunity. This is where I begin to get frustrated. Life insurance is so misunderstood, even by the financial masters, that it's no wonder people raise their eyebrows when I recommend it.

Why do I recommend life insurance? Because it's the most efficient way to protect your family's financial security. Is it a waste of money?

Only if you do it the way people in the financial industry—even the insurance companies—recommend. But if you do it the right way, life insurance provides protection for your family, very attractive appreciation potential, significant tax benefits, and financial flexibility like no other financial products. That's why nearly everyone should *want* life insurance, even if they plan to defy mortality.

But it's tough to convince people of those advantages. Further into the book—in the Five Things You Can Do with Your Money section—I'll go into more detail about the reasons why you would want life insurance in your investment universe.

Injured With No Income: Disability Insurance in Detail

Other than death, the most significant risk to your family's financial stability is the inability to earn an income due to a disability. Many people think disability insurance would only apply to them if they were, say, a surgeon who needed to protect against the risk of a disease or injury, which would then prevent them from performing surgeries. This is only one of many scenarios where disability insurance would be needed. Illnesses, heart attack, even back pain and arthritis are significant causes of disability.

Why do you need it? Can your family live on $1,065 a month? That is the average monthly benefit paid by Social Security Disability Insurance (SSDI). Statistically, you are more likely to suffer a disability than a serious loss on your home, but nearly everyone has homeowner's insurance. Disability insurance is one of the most important types of insurance, yet only an estimated 44 percent of workers in the United States have it. Why? Cost is a main reason people avoid considering coverage, even though the average person can expect to pay only 1–3 percent of their annual income. When looking at a comprehensive protection plan of all your assets, remember that your ability to work and bring in an income is the greatest asset you have to protect.

The important question to ask is not, "Will it happen to me?" It's, "Could your family meet its financial obligations if you became sick or hurt?" If the answer is no, then you should consider the addition of a supplemental disability policy to your financial plan. Disability insurance is NOT the same as workers' compensation insurance, but many people tend to mistake one for the other. Less than 5 percent of disability claims are due to a work-related accident.

If we think of a financial plan as a roadmap to a destination, the fuel of the financial plan is your income. Without income, the plan stops in its tracks. It's the equivalent of your car running out of gas. You can't go anywhere. If you are unable to earn income, how can you have a successful financial plan? How can you reach your financial goals— retire at age 65, pay for your kid's college, travel—if you don't have income? Disability insurance protects you against the loss of income, against running out of gas. It keeps you on the road to your financial destination.

You should protect as much of your income as you can. The fact is, most of us will find ourselves financially struggling if we are sick or hurt and unable to work. With many health insurance programs today, we are paying more and more out of pocket. Between keeping your monthly bills up to date and paying for added medical expenses, the money runs out fast. Feeling that you are protected if anything should happen to you is another step in the direction of a financially successful life.

Rob, a colleague of a friend, developed ALS (Lou Gehrig's disease) when he was just thirty years old. He was a police officer on his way to become a SWAT team member. Rob also taught martial arts, and he was an avid extreme skier and dirt-bike enthusiast. Rob was not the type of person to expect an illness of any kind; he was more likely to hurt himself from all of his other high-risk activities, as he had somewhat of an "invincibility" state of mind. Rob was enjoying life as a newlywed when his symptoms started. He began to lose his ability to walk, and eventually lost his ability to feed and bathe himself. Rob struggled mightily with being disabled, he felt so helpless. He had always been strong and healthy and able to take care of himself and others. During the difficult physical and emotional battle with his illness, Rob had some peace of mind that his family's day-to-day needs were being met. Two years later he died from the disease. His medical coverage helped with some of the bills related to his health, but the disability payments he received from his coverage at work really helped replace some of his income in his family's time of need.

Disability income will protect your financial plan, and ensure that you have resources to achieve your goals and fulfill your role as provider for your children. Some people leave their financial futures to chance. Here are some statistics that might inspire you to take some action and create an efficient financial plan that includes disability insurance, since it's the insurance you're most likely to need and use.

- One in eight workers will be disabled for five years or more during their working careers.

- The average long-term disability claim lasts 31.2 months.

Still not convinced? I can give you even scarier numbers:

- In the last 10 minutes, 498 Americans became disabled.

- Approximately 90 percent of disabilities are caused by illnesses rather than accidents (see Common Terms and Examples of Disability Claims Diagnoses list).

- Stroke is a leading cause of a serious long-term disability.

- 90 percent of Americans underestimate their own chances of becoming disabled.[1]

After you consider those sobering figures, consider your possible sources of assistance if you are disabled. Remember Workers' Compensation will pay only if you are injured on the job, and it pays only

---

1. Sources: 2010 Gen Redisability Fact Book, Commissioners' Disability Insurance Tables A and C, assuming equal weights by gender and occupation class, National Safety Council®, Injury Facts® 2008 Ed., 2010 Council of Disability Awareness, Centers for Disease Control and Prevention.

medical bills. If you think the government will take care of you if you suffer a disability, here is the Social Security Administration's definition of disability:

> *The inability to engage in any substantial gainful activity by reason of any medically determinable physical or mental impairment which has lasted or could be expected to last for a continuous period of 12 months or result in death. Impairment must be so severe that the individual is unable to engage in substantial, gainful work that exists in the immediate area in which the applicant lives.*

In 2009, 65 percent of initial SSDI claims through the government were denied. Trying to meet the definition above is very difficult. Many people have to complete mountains of forms to apply, only to be denied and have to reapply again. Many of you may have disability coverage through your employer, and that's great; however, you should still consider looking at your situation to determine if you have a need for supplemental coverage. If an employer pays for your disability policy, the benefits are usually taxable. If you pay for the policy, the benefits are usually tax-free.

People are beginning to favorably view the advantages of supplemental disability insurance, as touted by the ubiquitous AFLAC duck on television commercials.

More people should pay attention and investigate their disability insurance options.

Some people look at the cost of disability insurance, as with many other types of insurance, as if it would be a mistake to spend that money. Humans tend to think they are invincible: "It's a waste of money, I won't ever need it." Or, "I have enough money in other investments to cover my family if I could not work for a bit," or "It will never happen to me." We work hard for a large part of our lives to build up a fruitful financial portfolio, we want to live life to the fullest when we retire, and we may want to pass along a bit of wealth to our children. To achieve this final destination you must protect what you built or are building.

As with all insurance, disability policies come in all shapes and sizes. Picking the right policy will require some guidance from professionals who are familiar with the range of products offered.

Long-Term Care Insurance

For some people, your assets and income may be enough that if you should ever need long-term care services, you would have plenty of money to pay for those costs out of pocket. For others, your assets may be smaller, that if you should ever need long-term care services you may be eligible for medical assistance. And for those in the middle, you've probably been saving to obtain a certain lifestyle for your retirement years. You may have too much in assets to qualify for medical assistance without spending down to the state poverty levels, but you do not have enough money to afford a potential care event of two to three years without it becoming a financial hardship.

Reports show that if you reach the age of 65, the likelihood of needing long-term care services for some period at some time in your life is 70 percent. As a nation, we're living longer than we ever have, and we're living with ailments that may have killed us even five and ten years ago. And with that comes the fact that health care is not only more expensive, but we're also paying for it for more years than ever, and having more expensive procedures toward the end of life.

Consider long-term care insurance as a way to protect your assets. When you need care, the insurance company will be paying the expenses, and you're protecting your assets so they're used in the manner you want to fund your retirement lifestyle.

More importantly, long-term care insurance is a means to protect your family. Many of us take for granted that we have spouses, children, or even grandchildren who love us so much they would be willing to put their needs aside to care for us when we need it. Is that what we want them to do? To give up their careers, move closer to us or have us move closer to them, forgo family vacations, kids' activities, etc., just so they can be the ones to take care of us? Many of us do not want that; we want our children and grandchildren to enjoy their lives and we do not want to be a burden to them. Why then would they do it? Because they love us.

However, we do want our children to visit us and make sure our care is provided appropriately, but not to have them physically care for us. Imagine that you have lived a healthy life, you are now ninety, and need some help with your day-to-day activities; your "plan" was to have your children care for you. But now your children are in their sixties and seventies, and they might also need care. Do we really want to have to rely on our grandchildren to help us with our activities of daily living? I don't think so.

Long-term care insurance is about control. It can protect your independence and it allows you to get care in the manner in which you choose.

If you do consider long-term care insurance for all of the reasons listed, some things to look for in a policy would include:

- Inflation protection—so your benefit amount grows over time

- Comprehensive coverage—so care is given at home, adult day care centers, assisted living facilities, nursing homes, and memory care centers

- Waiver of premiums—so when you are receiving your benefits, you will not pay premiums

- Shared care plans—when two people share in coverage, the likelihood of the policy benefits being used becomes greater

- Consider purchasing policies while you are in your fifties to early sixties. You are more likely to get coverage, and premiums tend to be quite a bit less expensive.

Consider…what are the consequences to me and my family by owning a long-term care policy, and never needing it?

Consider…what are the consequences to me and my family by *not* owning a long-term care insurance policy, and needing it?

The bottom line is this: If you can afford the cost of a long-term care policy without any detraction from your lifestyle, you should seriously consider buying it.

Part of a Plan

In this discussion of insurance, I've treated each type of insurance as a separate entity. But they should be reviewed and looked at in terms of your overall financial plan, and in combination with all other components of your plan. I recommend life insurance and disability insurance for most people, but your life situation and your goals will dictate whether they should be a part of your plan. As in all other aspects of financial planning, you cannot examine one variable in isolation. Planning for emergencies is but one consideration. You cannot spend your life and all your money waiting for catastrophe. You have to live for today, and for tomorrow, too.

In the next chapter section we'll take a look at a much happier topic: planning to improve your life. Your love for others, your spouse, and perhaps children will be expressed by your plans to help them live full lives even if you do not. But your love for others will also be expressed in sharing the joys of living, and the unique contributions you make to their lives every day by being who you are.

Do we need to look the worst case in the face and plan for it? Yes. Do we need to be consumed by it? Never.

Plan for the certainty of uncertainty, but expect, and also plan for, the best.

Planning to Improve Your Life

Financial planning is not a drab endeavor that requires you to live a Spartan lifestyle for the next thirty years so that you won't end up living on the streets when you are seventy,, with all your possessions in a shopping bag. There is more to life than waiting for a disaster–or retirement.

Quality-of-life issues also require planning. Expand your horizons, have fun, acquire new skills. You have a lot of life to be lived between now and when you walk away from your job for the last time. People forget to plan for their lives in the short term. Maybe you want to see Paris before you need a walker. Maybe you want to cliff dive in Acapulco, which might not be a good idea if you've already reached retirement age. Or maybe you want to take a cooking class now with Chef Luigi that will give you hours of pleasure for the rest of your life, instead of later when you might be on a restricted diet.

Your goals for saving and investing don't have to be limited to three or four decades down the road.

A good plan takes into account how you want to live now, as well as later in life, balancing between now and then. Are you living a humdrum life now so that you won't have to when you're older? That depends on your goals. Maybe sacrificing now, living a no-frills lifestyle, will enable you to have the money to do things you want to do when you retire. However, it is important to realize that you might be less healthy then.

A friend in his late fifties spends as much time as possible with his year-old grandchild, often devoting entire days to her. He lights up when he talks about her. In a quiet moment, he admitted he treasures the hours with her because when his own daughters were growing up, he traveled constantly while establishing his career. Now he has a second chance to experience the joys of watching a child grow minute by minute. Not everyone gets a "do over" for such moments.

Even though I made negative comments earlier about our propensity to consume, you should not pinch pennies for some distant day. A good plan takes into account how you want to live now and later, and strikes a balance between being prudent and super-frugal now so you don't have to later. By curtailing frivolous spending now, you may reap the benefits in one or two instead of twenty-five years.

Often the best investments we can make are in ourselves. We can improve our quality of life by pursuing a passion or hobby. We can improve our earning potential by investing in education or professional credentials. We can sometimes do both by investing in our own business.

How can you plan to enjoy life more? Your enjoyment or mine or another guy's are likely to be so vastly different. Dream a little and balance the future with the present. I've always liked this thought from a preschool teacher I know. Every morning she had her students say when they arrived in class: "This is the day we have. We can use this day or throw it away, but this is the day we have." What a wonderful way to ingrain in children the notion that they can make of each day what they want. They are each responsible for how their day turns out. We adults are, too.

Remember John Lennon's famous line: "Life is what happens while we're making other plans." Don't let that happen to you while you're making your financial plan. Include the present in your plan so that life doesn't pass you by.

Planning for Retirement

When the topic is money, few things command our attention as much as planning for retirement. Part of that has to do with our culture in the United States. We worship youth, and our elderly are often pushed aside to fend for themselves. Extended family isn't what it used to be in this country, but it still is in many other nations.

We also are consumed by our work and our careers. When we meet people, one of the first questions is, "What do you do?" In many parts of Europe, that rarely comes up in conversation. We define ourselves by our work, and spend longer hours working than do people in most other countries. We work longer days, longer weeks, and take shorter vacations. Perhaps it's no wonder that so many people are eager for retirement–and worried whether they will have sufficient incomes to live the way they hope to without working.

Despite all the time we spend thinking and talking about saving and investing for retirement, Americans are notoriously bad savers. Our saving rate pales in comparison to saving rates in other countries.

The only place to begin to tackle this subject, so fraught with expectation, is with how much you should save or invest to retire in the style you desire.

Wants versus Needs

Most discussions of retirement planning begin with an estimate that you will need 70 percent of your working income when you retire. That's the wrong place to start.

Don't let anyone tell you what you might need in retirement. You start the discussion by telling them what you want.

What's the point of planning, saving, and investing? If you begin where many industry experts and consultants advise, you may already be planning to fail. Don't start with *needs* planning. Needs planning is very popular, and is the prevalent planning methodology in the financial industry today. It's one of the worst things you could do—and suggests a financial outlook that I'm constantly fighting. If you base your planning on what you need, you are aiming too low. In the late 1960s, the Rolling Stones sang, "You can't always get what you want." But why would anyone plan for anything less?

The Eeyore School of Financial Planning

If you don't have young kids around, you may have forgotten about Eeyore, the donkey in the wonderful Winnie the Pooh books. Eeyore walks around with a cloud over his head, always pessimistic. Eeyore's philosophy of life is, "If something can go wrong, it probably will." The world is full of needs planners, and their alma mater was the Eeyore School of Financial Planning.

Here's how needs planning works: You decide that it is time to plan for your retirement. You make $50,000 a year working and, following traditional financial thinking, decide that you need 70 percent of that income for retirement. Therefore, instead of $50,000, you decide you will need $35,000. Now that's a "Gloomy Place," as Eeyore's meadow is called.

At retirement, your cost of living may be lower than ever, but isn't that the time to enjoy the fruits of your years of labor? How much fun can you have on $35,000 per year? My point is this: You may *need* only $35,000 per year, but how much do you *want*?

**Your financial plan should be designed
to help you get what you want, not just what you need.**

Why limit yourself to your perceived need rather than realizing your full financial potential? You should attempt to determine accurately your need, and then exceed it. If you're embarking on a 100-mile car trip and your car gets twenty miles per gallon, you need five gallons of gas in your tank. My advice, however, would be to completely fill your tank before you leave. What if you encounter a traffic jam, a detour, or bad weather?

Needs planning is based on several assumptions that you are "average"—and we have already established that you are not, and do not want to be.

False Assumption #1: You'll Spend Less in Retirement

How exactly will you spend less in retirement? Maybe you will if you are happy to sit at home year round and read books borrowed from the library. Most people, however, have big plans for retirement, the first time in their adult lives that they can do precisely what they want to do. They plan to travel, play golf whenever they feel like it, and pursue their hobbies. But all of those activities require money—probably more money than you'll save by not having workrelated expenses.

Even social life changes for many people when they retire. The social camaraderie of the workplace is gone. To make up for it, people get together with friends more often. But where do they go? They meet for lunch or dinner—and probably spend more on eating out in retirement than ever before.

Many people assume as well that they'll spend less on possessions. After all, don't they already own the furniture, the TV, and all their kitchen appliances? True, but what of the next generation of technological advances? Will you want to upgrade your computer so you can watch movies on it—any movie, any time—and use it as a videophone to talk to and watch your grandchildren? Or will you be content to stick with older technology?

Technology advancements and planned obsolescence will certainly continue to change everyone's lives. Think of our many "necessities" today that yesterday were luxuries. When did telephones become a necessity? When will portable or cellular phones be viewed the same as old rotary telephones once were? What new conveniences will become commonplace in the next ten or twenty years? Will you keep up to date? Will it matter? To most people it will, and they will buy the new conveniences. That takes money.

Before you plan to retire on an income that is based on a needs-planning target of 70 percent of your income, I challenge you to do some calculating. If you're making $50,000 now, as in our example above, and plan to retire on $35,000, figure out how you are going to spend $15,000 less every year. Your Golden Ager's discount at movie theaters is not going to cut your cost of living by 30 percent.

False Assumption #2: Your Housing Costs Will Be Much Lower in Retirement

If your mortgage is paid off, your housing costs could drop significantly. That will be true for many people who have lived in the same house for the past three decades and paid for it, which today is quite uncommon. But even that is no guarantee that your housing costs are going to plummet. Maintenance on older homes is ongoing, and property taxes may increase. Some people have had to sell their homes because their retirement income wasn't high enough to pay the property taxes. They had the "misfortune" of owning a home in a desirable neighborhood where property values skyrocketed, and their property taxes followed. And while they may have made some money by selling their houses, they loved their homes and neighborhoods and found it painful to leave. The housing bubble that precipitated the 2008 financial crisis added a new issue. Many people are underwater on their mortgages; some are walking away from their homes and others will never be able to sell for the potential value. With the sure-thing mentality of home ownership a thing of the past, people moving into retirement need to include a plan for managing housing costs into their overall financial planning.

Wants Planning: Realize Your Potential

Needs planning is great advice for the masses—those who have no plan now and need some place to start. It's a great way to convince people that they should save something, but it's pitiful advice for people who want to do better than "get by." Don't settle for mediocrity in your investment planning.

Try to excel. It is fine to set a minimum for what you'll need to get by, but then aim a little higher—and plan to get there. Become a "wants" planner.

Many of my clients retire with higher annual incomes than when they were working. Don't be satisfied to be one of the "70 percenters"— people striving, to use the word lightly, to retire at 70 percent of their working income just because they have been brainwashed to believe that's what they'll need.

What Do You Want?

Instead of planning to meet your needs based on some percentage of your working income, ask yourself what you want from life: What life have you imagined? What is your dream? Few people hesitate when asked about their dream. For some, the dream is a secure retirement, perhaps early, with the time, comfort, and good health to enjoy family and friends. Others imagine the opportunity to pursue passions: art, music, travel, perhaps even the infuriating white-dimpled ball or the wily walleye. Perhaps you also dream of providing education and security for your children or grandchildren, leaving a legacy in your community, or improving life for future generations.

Your financial plan begins with your dreams, because they are the true currency of your life.

The whole purpose of financial planning is to provide adequate resources so that people don't have to pinch pennies. How much will be enough for you? That depends on your lifestyle, your dreams, and, in most cases, the people you love.

Don't Settle for Half a Plan

Once you have determined what you want in retirement, you have made a good start. You at least know where your financial plan has to take you. And then you start investing to accumulate as much money as possible to help you get to some magical figure that will provide the income you have chosen. Well, yes, partly. That's one-third of a financial plan.

Everyone focuses on how they can accumulate enough assets to carry them from retirement until they die, but almost no one thinks about how they will distribute those assets. Think about these questions:

- What impact will distribution have on how and how much you save and invest?

- How will you liquidate your investments?

- Will there be costs associated with that?

- What will be the impact of taxes on your distributions?

- Will you be in a higher or a lower tax bracket?

- Will you be taxed at ordinary income tax rates or capital gains tax rates?

- If you die before your spouse, will your spouse collect life insurance?

- How will that affect the distribution of other assets?

- Will there be anything left for your estate? What will the tax bite on those assets be for your heirs?

There are three phases of financial planning: accumulation, distribution, and legacy. All three are needed for a complete plan for most people. Problems arise because one cannot devise an efficient distribution strategy after the fact. In other words, the way you accumulate assets very often determines how they can be distributed. Efficient distribution strategies can't undo some steps taken years earlier. By the time you retire, you may have to live with the results of your accumulation strategy.

- Example: A sixty-three-year-old man came to our firm for assistance in planning distributions from his IRA. He did not anticipate needing to use his IRA funds for the foreseeable future. He wanted to know if he should delay distribution until age 70½ when the IRA requires it. We recommended that he begin to take distributions from his IRA at the most advantageous tax rates, and also to factor in the likely appreciation of his IRA before he reached age 70½. If his IRA continued to appreciate at historical average rates for equities—over 8 percent a year—his IRA would nearly double in value before he reached age 70½. Many seniors have found that those types of returns, in the time between retirement and mandatory distribution, push their income from an IRA into a higher tax bracket—which really defeats the purpose of tax-deferred accounts. We determined that the potential appreciation could push his income into a higher tax bracket, and recommended that he begin taking distributions annually to "soak up" his present tax bracket. He began immediately to take distributions from his IRA to the extent that it would push his income to the highest level of his present tax bracket without pushing him into a higher one.

Just to illustrate the point, let's assume that the top of his tax bracket was $50,000 in income. If he anticipated income from other sources to be $35,000, he would want to take a distribution from his IRA of $15,000. He would gradually reduce his IRA account that way so that he could reduce the likelihood that mandatory distributions from his IRA would push his income above $50,000 in later years. In addition, he shifted assets into personal accounts, which may not be subject to taxes when he dies.

Why don't more people plan for all three phases of their financial lifecycle—accumulation, distribution, and legacy? The answer is found partly in our country's financial institutions. They make their money largely from selling you products, and taking commissions on helping you accumulate assets. Far fewer of them provide much assistance with distribution or legacy. The services they do provide in those fields are targeted primarily at the very rich. The reason is fairly simple: It takes considerably more expertise to provide good advice on distribution and legacy strategies. Anyone can recommend a "hot" stock. Devising an efficient distribution strategy is quite a bit more complicated, and requires a great deal more knowledge.

Of course, all three phases of a financial plan are determined by individual values and goals. There is no such thing as a universal plan. Be very skeptical about any advice that is given as "appropriate" for everybody. No financial instrument fits everyone's needs.

Now let's take a closer look at some of the most widely used tools to save and invest for retirement. Most people will retire with assets in some mixture of these types of retirement accounts. Diversify your retirement accounts as much as you want to diversify your holdings within investment accounts.

The greater diversification you have within your retirement plan, the greater the distribution options you are likely to have, even if you wait until you are just about retired to create a distribution strategy.

Social Security

Social Security is the one form of retirement investment in which we all participate. Social Security reaches almost every family, and at some point will touch the lives of nearly all Americans. And even if Social Security is overhauled in the near or distant future, it is likely to remain a universal program, meaning everyone will participate in some form. Every working American pays Social Security taxes. Approximately 17.5 percent of the entire United States population receives some sort of monthly Social Security benefit, and that rate will increase as the more than 76 million American Baby Boomers (1946–1964) start retiring in droves–about 10,000 per day will be eligible.

Social Security originally came into being and was signed into law by President Franklin Delano Roosevelt on August 14, 1935. The reason for his action was the Great Depression, and the need it created in the United States for government intervention. Social Security was the first federal government program that dealt with the economic security of its citizens by creating a social insurance program that has helped to keep millions of Americans out of poverty.

Social Security offers protection four different ways: disability, survivor's benefits, retirement benefits, and Medicare health insurance. Roughly 8.6 million people currently receive Social Security disability benefits, and more than 6.3 million Americans receive survivor benefits.

Social Security is funded by you and your employer; 6.2 percent by your employer and 4.2 percent of a worker's gross salary is deducted from his or her paycheck. This is known as FICA. Medicare tax is 4.45 percent by you and your employer. Social Security taxes go into two different trust funds: 85 cents of every dollar pays present monthly benefits to retirees and their families, and 15 cents of every dollar pays present benefits to the disabled and their families. Surplus dollars *not used* to pay administrative expenses or benefits are invested in U.S. government securities. These dollars are intended to be available to pay benefits in the future.

As you work and pay taxes, you earn Social Security credits. You get one credit for each $1,130 in earnings up to a maximum of four credits per year in 2012. Most people need forty credits to qualify for retirement benefits, or ten years of employment. It's the earnings, though, and not the number of credits, that determine your overall Social Security retirement benefit. Your benefit is based on your date of birth, your type of benefit, your Social Security number, and your earnings over your working lifetime.

The following formula is used to calculate future Social Security benefits:

Step 1: List compensation under Social Security wage base for each year worked.

Step 2: Adjust each year's wages for inflation.

Step 3: Determine the average indexed adjusted monthly earnings based on the number of years in Step 1.

Step 4: Multiply your average indexed adjusted monthly earnings by percentages in a formula specified by law.

The result of this formula is your primary benefit amount or the amount you are eligible to receive at full retirement age.

Those over age sixty receive a statement of their projected benefits sometime around their birthday each year. Others can go to **www. socialsecurity.gov** to access their statement online. Many services are also offered online.

Social Security was never intended to be anyone's sole source of retirement income. The more you earned in your working life, the higher your payment. Social Security is intended to replace about 53 percent of income for low-wage earners, about 40 percent for average-wage earners, about 32 percent for high-wage earners, and about 24 percent for those who earn more than the maximum wage base.

To retire and be eligible for Social Security benefits you must be fully insured, meaning you have at least forty credits, be at least age sixty-two, and have filed an application for retirement benefits. Another thing that many Social Security recipients do not realize prior to receiving benefits is that Social Security benefits may be taxable.

If you are an individual income tax filer, and one half of your Social Security benefits plus other taxable income sources and municipal bond interest exceeds $25,000 per year (married filing jointly increases this amount to $32,000), 50 to 85 percent of your benefits may be included in your taxable income, taxed at your ordinary income tax rate.

- If you file a joint return, and your combined income exceeds $32,000, but is less than $44,000, again, you may be taxed on up to 50 percent of your Social Security benefit at your ordinary income tax rate.

- If you're a single filer, and your income exceeds $34,000, or if you're a joint filer and your combined income exceeds $44,000, up to 85 percent of Social Security benefits may be taxed at your ordinary income tax rate.

The benefits you receive from Social Security were never intended to replace your working income or be your sole source of income at retirement, and with the benefits incurring significant income tax liability for many people, almost all Americans need to have alternative sources of retirement income. You must save and invest for your own future. Americans need much more than just Social Security. You cannot depend on the government to give you your full retirement income—regardless of how Congress adjusts or changes Social Security now or in the future.

Tax-Deferred Plans in Detail: Beware Again

One way that you may be planning for retirement is through a tax-deferred retirement plan. They are the primary vehicle for retirement investing these days. IRAs, SEPs, Keoghs, and 401(k)s all allow you to invest money in a retirement plan and defer taxes on that money until you withdraw it. The assumption is that when you withdraw that money, supposedly in retirement, you will have less income and you may, therefore, have to pay a lower tax rate on that money. Don't count on it.

In my opinion, we rely far too heavily on pretax plans, which suffer from two potential problems:

1. Failure to consider a distribution strategy; and

2. Tax rates that are currently at historic lows, and are more likely to rise than fall.

What you have to keep in mind is that the taxes on these retirement accounts are deferred, but they are not tax-free. Although they do not count against your income when earned, and any earnings on those assets also are not taxed when earned, you will have to pay taxes on those assets and earnings when they are withdrawn from the account, usually in retirement. In many cases, even your heirs will have to pay a tax when they receive the balance after you die.

The prevailing wisdom is that you should take full advantage of these plans to the extent that you are eligible. In other words, everyone should invest the maximum allowed, which varies from one plan to another. Look at the reduction you can get in taxes immediately. What more do you want?

Maximizing your retirement account is certainly worth considering, but many people should reject those plans because for them, pretax retirement plans are a very *inefficient* strategy to achieve their financial goals.

While many self-anointed experts who get time on TV or space in newspapers consider my position (outlined below) blasphemous, my question to them is, "How can the same financial solution apply equally well to everyone's financial situation?" The answer is simple: It doesn't!

How did society get to the point where virtually everyone believes we should pour our money into pretax retirement plans? To answer that question, consider who benefits if we all follow that course of action.

Contributions to these plans, by their design and because of tax treatment, remain in place for a very long time. If you begin making contributions while you're in your thirties, you're unlikely to take any distributions until you're age 59½ or older. The custodian of the money has the account for twenty, thirty, even forty years. Do banks, insurance companies, mutual fund companies, brokerage houses, and other financial institutions like this arrangement? Of course. Think how they can use that money over that length of time. Do you think they might devote some of their marketing budget to convincing investors that these accounts are good? I think it's safe to conclude that financial institutions love pretax retirement accounts, and spend a great deal of money convincing the public that they should love them, too.

But are they really such a great deal? Let's look at their supposed advantages—which for many people can turn out to be disadvantages.

Presumed Advantage #1: Tax-Deferred Plans Avoid Taxes

Many people tell me they participate in these plans to avoid taxes. But they don't avoid taxes at all. They simply defer taxes until that income is received. You can pay now or you can pay later—but you will pay.

Presumed Advantage #2: You Will Be in a Lower Tax Bracket in Retirement

The assumption is that when the income is actually received, and the tax on the income is due, the investor will likely be retired and in a lower tax bracket. That may be true for people who plan to have 70 percent of their working income in retirement, however, I think you should set a higher target. The only reason for being in a lower tax bracket in retirement is that you didn't save and plan for retirement as well as you could have.

But even the assumption is faulty that with a reduction in income, you will also be in a lower tax bracket. If you're married, and together you and your spouse have a combined taxable income of $120,000 per year while working, you're in the 25 percent Federal tax bracket. Following the needs-planning strategy promoted by graduates of the Eeyore School of Financial Planning, the outlook is always gloomy: You would then strive to retire at 70 percent of your working income, or $84,000 a year. Now we'll check our tax tables and—whoops—that's still in the 25 percent Federal tax bracket. By following the prevailing wisdom, you would retire with 30 percent less income but still be in the same tax bracket. Where's the advantage in that?

Furthermore, how do we know what future tax rates will be? We don't and there is a lot of margin for error. What we do know is that the highest marginal tax rate, which is 35 percent as of this writing, is toward the low end of their historical range of 7 percent to a high of 94 percent.

Do you trust politicians to continue to try to balance budgets or pay off our rapidly growing national debt? I suspect that even if budgets are balanced, our debt won't be paid down very soon.

- What happens if the recovery rate of our economy slows?

- What happens if the recovery fizzles completely?

- Will growth projections be as rosy as some would have us believe?

- Will economic growth pull us out of this deficit, or do you think Congress might be tempted to raise taxes? It's the quickest way to increase revenues.

While we don't know what future tax rates will be, we do know we presently have very low rates compared to the past, and that government spending outpaces revenues. Would you bet that your future tax rate will be higher or lower than it is now? My bet is higher—for all of us.

If tax rates go up, deferring tax on your pretax retirement plan may be counterproductive. Even if you are not in a higher tax bracket in the future, but retire with income in the same tax bracket that you are currently in, you have little advantage to delaying the tax.

Presumed Advantage #3: You Have an Immediate Gain through Tax Deferral

Another misconception with regard to pretax retirement plans is that the tax savings are somehow available to you. For example, in a 25 percent Federal tax bracket, a $5,000 contribution to an IRA would save $1,250 in taxes. But that savings doesn't come to you; it's in the plan and it is hard to access without penalty, and that remains true until you reach age 59½. You can't use that money—not for your cost of living, not even for investments beyond the narrow range of equity investments that most plans offer. In truth, your spendable income has decreased by $3,750, because you had to spend $5,000 to save the $1,250.

If you are putting all of your investable income into your pretax retirement plan, what will happen if you have a family emergency that requires you to withdraw it? You may pay a 10 percent penalty, plus the full amount withdrawn (even the 10 percent paid in penalty) can be taxed as income in the year it is withdrawn. Or what if you come up with a great idea for a business, but you need money to get it off the ground? No, you can't withdraw from your pretax retirement plan without paying the penalty.

Pretax retirement plans offer almost no flexibility. They were designed for one thing only: to encourage people to create a nest egg for retirement.

The effect of some people's contributions to pretax plans is that they live as if they are poor now so they won't have to live as if they are poor later. That's not a very appealing tradeoff, especially if other retirement planning strategies are available that may not force such a drastic choice. Sure, an effective investment strategy and retirement plan may require some sacrifices in the shorter term, but they should be balanced against an expected reward. And those sacrifices will be reduced with an effective strategy for the future.

Here's the kicker to the story about a couple who had good income, but couldn't qualify for a home mortgage because they had more than $100,000 in credit card debt: They also had more than $400,000 in 401(k) plans. Their 401(k)s were doing pretty well, too, delivering a return of 8 percent a year. But that means they were *losing* 10 percent a year on their pretax retirement plans, because they were paying 18 percent on their credit card debt. Now *that's* a bad investment, and a cautionary tale for those who are scraping money together for their contribution to a pretax plan.

Here's one significant exception to my skepticism about the wisdom of pretax plans. If your employer matches what you put into the plan, it is too good to pass up for most people—at least up to the level that your employer will match. Many employers will match your contribution up to 3 to 4 percent of your income. Employers who do this calculate that contribution in determining your overall compensation, so it's really part of your pay. You should make every effort to qualify for that match, because your money immediately doubles, and you still get the tax deduction. Whether you contribute the maximum you are allowed, however, above any amount that your employer matches, requires careful scrutiny.

Who Needs Pretax Plans...

Pretax retirement plans do make sense for essentially three types of people—those who:

1. Have their contributions matched by their employer.

2. Are already in the highest tax brackets and have a reasonable chance of being in a lower tax bracket in retirement.

3. Do not have the discipline to save or invest without the plan. With all of the plan's shortcomings, for many people, pretax plans are still far better than saving and investing nothing.

...And Who Does Not

Everyone else, but especially those who:

1. Have any outstanding consumer debt. Pay it off before you contribute to a pretax plan.

2. Are saving for a down payment on a home. Your mortgage interest deduction will probably provide a bigger tax deduction than your pretax plan, even as you build equity in an asset and lock in your housing costs, which you can't do with rent.

3. Are disciplined savers and investors.

4. Invest in strategies that are tax-free, allow other tax deductions, or generate tax credits.

Summary of Pretax Plans

Without knowing the specifics of your situation, I can't say for sure whether your pretax retirement plan is the best way for you to save and invest. I can say with certainty, however, that pretax retirement plans:

- Do not actually avoid taxes. They merely defer taxes by deferring income.

- Provide no additional spendable income. The tax savings generated by the contribution are in the plan. In fact, spendable income actually decreases.

- Will not necessarily be taxed at a lower rate when distributed to you. We don't know what future tax rates will be. However, a compelling argument can be made that they are unlikely to be lower than they are now.

- Are heavily promoted by large financial institutions that benefit greatly by holding your money for a few decades.

- Are inefficient because your beneficiaries are also fully taxed.

Be sure to evaluate pretax retirement plans in the context of your overall financial picture. Is retirement saving and investing your top priority? On one hand, an early start to retirement planning can make an enormous difference. Other financial goals may take priority, however. Can you save to make a down payment on a house at the same time you're putting money into a retirement plan? How do you resolve competing priorities? These questions cannot be answered without considering your life situation, and the people you love.

Consider pretax plans alongside all other options for retirement planning. For most people pretax plans should not be the only investment vehicle for retirement.

Finally, maintain control over pretax accounts after leaving a job. You can take it with you, and you should. If you leave it behind with a former employer, the managers of those funds may make decisions you don't like. Shift the account to your control, and make the decisions yourself—or with your financial advisor.

Two tools whose value may justify the cost

Variable annuities and permanent life insurance can be very effective tools in a financial plan. They cost more than other growth investments, which is why they are often overlooked, but they provide value that may justify the cost.

They may provide better returns than other growth investments because the managers of those funds do not face some of the same market pressures that mutual fund managers face. They provide easy and inexpensive ways to rebalance your portfolio. And they both offer distinct advantages for estate planning.

If you are currently invested only in tax-deferred retirement accounts, I would strongly encourage you to also consider the Roth IRA. You do not get a tax deferment on your contributions to a Roth IRA, but the earnings in your investment account do accumulate tax-deferred. A Roth IRA is an excellent complement to traditional tax-deferred accounts for four reasons that differentiate them from traditional IRAs:

1. The earnings grow free from Federal tax.

2. You can withdraw your contributions penalty-and tax-free at any time.

3. There are no minimum required withdrawals starting at age 70½, so you can leave your money in as long as you want.

4. You have a wide range of investment options.

Roth IRAs are complicated, however, so don't make any decisions without talking to a financial professional.

Plan Together

The first step in planning for retirement with your spouse is to reach agreement on your primary objectives. Without that, a strategy is impossible, or at least a lot more complicated.

Often I've interviewed new client couples who are creating a financial plan, and they have fundamental disagreements on what they want from retirement. Sometimes they don't even realize their differences until I ask them both to write down their ideal retirement. I get back one piece of paper from Mars and one from Venus.

As in all other things with your spouse, communicate clearly and never assume. Lay out precisely what each of you wants, and decide how you can make those desires work together. Be specific. One couple was confident they shared a similar vision of retirement, a home on the beach. Only with my probing, we learned that he wanted to live in Florida and she wanted to live on Martha's Vineyard. Both were shocked, and neither would budge. They had always talked about a beach home, but had never gotten around to specifying which beach.

As part of your financial plan review, you might also want to confirm that your partner's plans or wants have not changed. You wouldn't want to find out years from now that your spouse decided long ago that his view of an ideal retirement had changed, but he had forgotten to tell you.

CHAPTER 2

Grown-up Advice on Money and Children

Careful and efficient financial planning has a clear impact on your children, and could help protect them financially in the event of your disability or death. It is also important for most people to pay for at least a portion of a child's education.

Perhaps the most important reason to plan, though, is the positive impact on your home life and your children, as it can reduce your worry about money. Moreover, if a financial advisor does much of the planning work, and the worrying, you will have more time to spend with your children. Wouldn't you rather have an expert figure out ways you can increase investable income, or reduce taxes, than spend tedious evening and weekend hours trying to decipher investment prospectuses and state and federal tax codes? You could be playing ball with your kids or getting to the recital early—and relaxed.

For example, a friend tells of the Saturday morning he spent with his five-year-old daughter. He was sitting on his front steps, contemplating his day's long to-do list, when his daughter came out and sat down next to him with a handful of pistachios. Before long they were setting nuts on the sidewalk, and watching chipmunks come up and snatch them. The little girl then filled a big oak leaf with nuts, calling it a "platter" at "Talia's Nut Restaurant." The two tried desperately to stifle their laughter so they wouldn't scare the chipmunks that were running up and stuffing their cheeks with nuts. Between chipmunk forays to the "platter," they watched a spider weaving a web in the railing on the steps. An hour and a half passed until the little girl turned to him and said, "Dad, this is the best day ever."

My friend's to-do list wasn't shortened that day—he never got to it, and he was glad he didn't. None of those chores could have ever resulted in the wonderful time he had with his daughter.

Money is about securing a future with innumerable "best days ever." And for so many of us, our children, or our prospective children, are a large part of our future.

Being the parent of two fantastic children is the most rewarding, challenging, and important aspect of my life. I would not trade the experience for anything. But economically, raising kids is the single greatest cost most of us will ever encounter. Boy, are they expensive: diapers, baby food, formula, candy, school, hobbies, and clothes, especially shoes, which they seem to outgrow every few weeks. The list is endless. And do you want to pay for their college education? Wedding? First car? First house? You will spend hundreds of thousands of dollars (some estimate as high as $222,000) in your lifetime for each child up through college graduation.

People without children have a huge economic advantage over the rest of us. However, the return on my investment in my children is incalculably high, as they've added immeasurably to the richness of my life. But children provide one of the most compelling reasons to create an efficient financial plan, not just for when you are still living, but also for transferring your wealth to them when you die.

The four key stages of your financial relationship with children will transform as they, and we, age. They are:

1. **Protector and provider:** What you provide for your children.

2. **Teacher:** What you teach your children. Intentionally or not, my wife and I, and many clients and colleagues,

have imparted our ideas about the role of money to our children. All parents are either eager or reluctant teachers—so good or bad, we are our children's role models.

3. **Financier:** What expenses you pay for your children. College—and more.

4. **Benefactor:** What you leave your children.

In almost all cases, as your children grow up, these stages and your roles overlap more. When you no longer provide for your children, you will remain, at least in your view, their protector—even if not financially. And you will always be a teacher. As they mature into adulthood, your children are often more willing to listen as you gradually grow wiser in their eyes. For some families, the financier stage might extend well beyond paying for some or all of their education.

5. **Financial Dependence:** A potential fifth stage in our money relationship with our children is best avoided—and can be with good planning and good fortune. That is when we as parents might need financial assistance from your children in our later years. (See the chapter on our financial relationship with our parents.)

The possibility that one may have to provide some economic assistance to parents is an important contingency in financial planning for many younger people. For those who are already elderly and facing financial burdens or obligations they cannot meet, financial planning can't achieve the same successes. As always, the time to plan is as soon as possible to avoid the challenges that arise when parents become financially dependent on their children.

Protector and Provider

In the developed world, we don't have to scrape and claw to keep our children clothed and fed. Our focus is on their comfort, helping them lead happy, productive lives instead of just staying alive.

I hope you will always be able to provide for your children until they can provide for themselves. It is better to plan than to hope. An important part of any financial plan is financial protection for your children if anything should happen to you. And then, there's one more essential piece of planning: planning for the unimaginable.

We always assume that if anything happens to us, at least our spouse will be able to raise our children and provide for them, ideally with the help of the financial protection we have left behind. But, heaven forbid, what happens if both you and your spouse are unable to provide for your children? As hard as it is, discuss that distant possibility with family or friends. Make arrangements, and put those designated names into your will of who has agreed to care for and protect your minor children, should you be unable.

A will is not simply a way to divide your assets, it is a way to designate disposition of your assets to care for your younger children. Equally important, it establishes your choice of legal guardians for your children and how your assets can be used for their benefit. It is difficult to imagine someone else raising your children. It is easier if you have made clear in a legal document your choice of loving, caring legal guardians.

Make a list of all the people you know whom you would trust to take care of your children. Close family, distant family, and close friends can all make excellent guardians, including families with whom your family is close, the families of your children's friends, even teachers or childcare providers. It's not about money. You can take care of the finances with what you leave, which is why you have life insurance. You can even instruct your trustee to provide funds for your chosen guardian to build an addition to their home or move to a larger home to accommodate your children.

Focus on finding a couple or person who would love your children as much as their own. Ask yourself which people on your list most closely share your religious beliefs, moral values, child-rearing philosophy, and educational and social values. Consider whether your candidates are patient, loving, affectionate role models, and if they're young, whether they're mature. If they're older, do they have the health, stamina, and desire to be the parents of young children? How would your kids get along with theirs, and are the two sets of children socially and intellectually well matched? Do they live close to other people who are important to your kids? And if the couple divorced, or one died, would you be comfortable with the one who was left?

Don't expect to find the perfect choice, but do trust your instincts. A couple that just feels right is probably better than one that meets all your criteria, but it doesn't feel quite right. Whatever your decisions, write down your reasons for them, so that if your choices are challenged in court, they'll stand up. Talk with everyone involved—the prospective guardians, of course—but also with your children if they're old enough. And get a good trust and estate lawyer to set up the money part so that both the guardians and your children don't ever have to worry about finances.

Teacher—a Never-ending Role

As a parent, you probably want your children to have a better life than you had growing up. It is a universal wish, and it is admirable.

If you are able to fulfill that wish, however, how do you:

- Instill ambition in your children, and keep them from getting spoiled?

- Teach them the value of what you earned, and to be good stewards of what you are able to give them?

- Raise financially smart children?

- Give them all you can without making them unwilling to be productive individuals?

Many parents, especially those blessed with affluence, fear that wealth will rob their children of ambition. According to a 2011 survey by U.S. Trust, 51 percent of high-net-wealth individuals said it is not important to leave their kids an inheritance, even though their children's success is an important measure of their own success.

One of my clients cashed out his stock in a dotcom startup, walking away with roughly $10 million after taxes. That didn't put him on the Forbes list of the richest people in the world. However, for his family, after years of toiling with little reward to get a business off the ground, it was an enormous sum. Before he and his wife told the kids anything, they wanted to have an estate plan in place, which was why they came to me. He was wondering when, or if, he'd ever tell his teenagers of this success.

The couple had gone through a lot of soul-searching about what to do with the money, and how it would best benefit their children, weighing the advantages against the harm that such a nest egg could do to their children's drive and ambition. This fact demonstrates that the couple has strong values, and has probably passed those values on to their kids—which means the kids will probably do well regardless of the parents' decision.

*I believe that too much money does not hurt children.
There's no such thing as too much money;
there's only too little character.*

Your role as teacher in all things financial begins with teaching your children about life, work and play, and, only then, where money fits in. The first lessons we give our children are the most important, and stay with them for life. We teach them how to love, we teach them values, and we teach them how to pursue their own happiness. If they learn those lessons well, they will find the appropriate place for money in their lives.

Most children are inclined to learn those invaluable lessons, but it takes time to teach the lessons. We often hear the phrase "quality, not quantity" in regard to time with our children. I disagree. Our children need quality *and* quantity.

The key is to invest time, as well as money, in your children's lives. You can't let devices and activities manage your children; you have to.

I believe that if you parent—if you love your children and tell them and show them by spending time with them—you can instill in them the character to handle the financial advantages you can give them.

Rules for Raising Responsible Kids

Here are three basic rules that parents should remember when teaching their children to understand the role of money in their lives, regardless of your financial circumstances.

Rule #1: Teach Values First

Whether you have a great deal of money or very little, your children have the same basic needs: security, love, and guidance in how to live in a diverse, ever-changing world.

If you teach values to your children—self-esteem; commitment to excellence; respect and concern for others; accountability to themselves, their community, school, faith community, and world—you certainly can teach them about money and its role in their lives. If you teach them values and set a solid foundation, they can learn to efficiently and responsibly use money, as well as the other tools they have.

Two concepts pervade every discussion I have about money: responsibility (using resources wisely) and finding what makes you happy (pursuing your own goals with passion). The same essentials apply to almost every childhood activity from school to play to spending money. You can never separate discussions of money from the core values you teach your kids because all are pieces of the same jigsaw puzzle.

Of course, to teach, you have to communicate effectively, which is the glue of all interpersonal relationships, whether with your spouse, parents, children, colleagues at work, or neighbors. Ineffective or inefficient communication nearly always plays a role in the breakdown of a relationship.

We need to pay equal attention to all three ways we communicate with our children: What We Do, How We Listen, and What We Say:

1) What We Do

Actions speak louder than words, and children are the world's best mimics. If you really want a confused kid, a kid who learns to distrust you, say one thing but do another. Our kids are learning our values even when we say nothing.

Showing our children our values begins with the big picture—how we live our lives. The priorities we set for ourselves are often the priorities our kids adopt. These lifestyle lessons require more thought than we often give them.

Your income, and how you earn it, are lessons in themselves for your children. How do your work life and income fit with your home life? How do you choose to balance the need to provide money for your family with the need to spend time with them? Very simply, that is the greatest complication in many financial plans. Creating a thoughtful financial plan forces you to focus on what your priorities are, and determines how money can help you achieve your goals. A good financial planning process tries to synchronize your values and your money, because the two are inextricably woven together. Some people mistakenly view financial planning as a way to have more money. On the contrary, some of the best financial plans I have helped to create were intended to help people live better on less money. Our goal was to align money and values.

My family is my top priority. When my family is happy, my clients are happy, and my employees are happy. I'm in a good place.

Our actions also include how we expose our children to the world beyond the narrow confines of our family, friends, and neighborhood.

To the extent we can, it's important that we help our children understand the wide range of people who live in our world. That may come through the books we read to them or the TV shows they watch. Our involvement in church, school, and community all demonstrate what we value. Diversity today usually refers to people of different races or ethnic backgrounds, but economic or financial diversity is also an important concept for kids to understand.

Our children have an advantage if they see the world not in narrowly defined groupings of race, class, and even religion, but in terms of many different types of individuals who live in many circumstances and make a wide variety of choices about how to live.

I've never forgotten where I came from, and I make sure that my kids understand that, too. When I was a child, we couldn't afford to take vacations. When you come from such humble beginnings, you never forget it, and you want to share that message with children. When we talk about our annual vacations, I remind our kids that we are fortunate. I try not to pound them with it, but want them to know that enjoying what money can buy is a privilege, not a right. For young children, it can be an eye-opener to learn that not every child has what they have or does what they do.

2) How We Listen

Listening is an especially important skill with children because their world is so immediate. But it's not only children; everybody wants to be heard. High-achieving, successful people must discipline themselves to take the time to truly listen to the members of their family, as the experience of being heard is critical to validating a child's personal worth.

One of our friends has a teenage son, and basically, the father is a good guy. However, he talks over everybody, believing what he has to say is more important than anyone else. His impatience shows when someone else is talking. He can hardly wait for that person to take a breath so he can jump in. Frequently he doesn't wait; he interrupts and takes over the conversation.

His son constantly shouts, even when alone. Is he shouting because his dad doesn't listen to him? Does he shout to be heard by his dad, who otherwise ignores him, and is too wrapped up in his own thoughts and words to listen to his child?

Your willingness to take time from your busy schedules to listen to your kids without criticism and without interruption gives their self-esteem an immeasurable boost.

Try to hear your words through a young child's ears. Do you ever hear yourself? Try this: Keep track of how many things you say that are positive, such as, "Oh, thank you so much for that, I appreciate your help," compared to negative things like, "I can't trust you," or "You're always talking too loud."

If we're honest about how we talk to others, we may be surprised by the number of interactions with our kids that are negative instead of positive. Self-esteem is built on the positives. That's not to say that parents shouldn't correct or discipline kids for inappropriate behavior. Discipline is most effective, however, when focused on the undesired behavior and conveyed in neutral terms. If you might now be quick to criticize, try to be more generous with praise.

3) What We Say

Even though your actions will speak louder than your words, kids need to hear the words, too. Consider carefully what you tell your children about money so they understand from the time they are very young what money can and cannot do for them, and how you believe it should and should not be used.

Parents should never substitute money and possessions for love and affection, but money can be a tool—a powerful teacher. Parents have to work together to answer some questions: What values do we want our children to learn? What will we provide for our children? What do we expect them to do in return? This is a parents-only discussion. Your decisions will determine what you say about money. Perhaps the two most important words are "yes" and "no"—your response to your kids' requests, demands, or pleadings that you buy them something. Don't be afraid to say no. But when you do say no, give them the real reason for your answer. When you say yes to your children's requests, don't be afraid to attach some strings to the generosity.

As an adult, two statements about money make a lot of sense, and have helped me come to grips with my own financial success—and have influenced what I tell my children about money.

1. "Make all you can, save all you can, give all you can."
    John Wesley, founder of the Methodist Church

2. "No one would remember the Good Samaritan if he'd only had good intentions. He had money as well." Former British Prime Minister Margaret Thatcher

Both quotes are powerful. Their point is that it matters what you do with your money, the values that guide your use of money. And implicit in both expressions is that money must be earned ethically and honorably.

I tell my children that they'll become what they think about, and I encourage them to think positively. Positive thoughts are the beginning of a chain that has been explained like this:

Watch your thoughts because your thoughts become your words. Watch your words because your words become your actions. Watch your actions because they become your habits. Watch your habits because they become your character. Watch your character because it becomes your destiny. —*Author unknown*

My Favorite Sayings

Almost every day I use phrases and expressions with my kids that I hope are reminders for them (and me) of how I want to live my life, and how I would like them to live their lives. My kids would probably roll their eyes because they hear them so often.

"No one can ruin your day without your permission. Make it a great day."

"The best way to escape a problem is to solve it."

"No excuses offered, none accepted."

"You can achieve what your mind can conceive."

"Cheaters never win, winners never cheat."

However, you should *not* tell your kids certain things, because such statements can have unintentional harmful effects on your children.

"We can't afford it."

How many times have we heard that? In addition to perhaps being dishonest, the response may cause unnecessary anxiety for small kids. If you're going to say no to something your child wants, be prepared to give the real reason. Don't just say, "We can't afford it." Tell them instead what you intend to spend your money on—even if it's the bills for gas, water, or electricity you use in your home.

What do you say to your kids when you know the "We can't afford it" excuse isn't true? You could give them everything their hearts desire—but more effective is getting them to imagine what they want to contribute to the world. Teach young children that no one gets everything he or she wants. Life is about making tough choices. Set expectations about what you can and can't provide or will or won't provide. As an example, a friend's fourteen-year-old daughter asked for a mobile phone. They could easily do that, but then they'd have no idea who she would be talking to. They were just not willing to do that, even though economically they could afford to get her a phone.

"We'll pay you for every A on your report card."

This is really a form of bribery, and sends the wrong message. Children should be taught to achieve goals for intrinsic reasons like self-satisfaction in achievement and a commitment to excellence—not for monetary rewards.

"Time is money."

It really isn't. Equating time spent on anything with its monetary value sends an unhealthy message that your time and your money are equal. We all know there is no substitute for time spent with your children. In fact, time in my life has a much higher value to me than money.

"They're disgustingly rich."

Or, as my parents used to say, "They were born with silver spoons in their mouths." Using words like "disgustingly" or "filthy" or "stinking" to describe someone's wealth encourages a child to see wealth negatively. And it isn't negative. If you or your parents were envious of anyone who had money, you might teach your children to be distrusting and resentful of people who had money and, frankly, to be intimidated by them.

Teaching your children that affluence is a bad thing is not only discriminatory and unfair, but could be detrimental to your child. The viewpoint could be an obstacle to your child's happiness and success, and the financial rewards that could come with it. It's far healthier to teach your children how to appreciate and be good stewards of whatever they may have in life. Will money make them happy? Certainly not. Will money come as a result of doing what *does* make them happy? Very possibly.

"Be thankful you don't live there."

This statement implies that happiness can't exist in a neighborhood or a house that isn't as comfortable as yours. It is the flip side of "disgustingly rich" comments. Teach your children to value human qualities rather than net worth or lifestyle, and they will be much happier and better able to adjust to any life circumstance. Money is neutral in terms of values, and can be used for good or bad. Neither having a lot of money nor having little money will make your children good or bad, happy or sad. They need to know this to have a healthy relationship with money–and they will learn it from listening to you.

Your children never have to learn to read stock tables or exchange rates to be wealthy or to use money efficiently. They do have to learn to work hard, have fun, save some of their money, and respect themselves and others. They have to learn values. It's worth repeating:

There's no such thing as too much money;
there's only too little character. It's our job as parents to
make sure our children have character. It's too important a
task to be left to others.

Rule #2: Teach Children the Joy of Work

You teach kids the joy of work, first, by enjoying work yourself. If you don't, it's probably time for a job change. Your kids need to see you excited about your own work and life. Your everyday actions speak far louder than any serious sit-down discussion about work and money, no matter how carefully and artfully you choose your words.

Second, I believe you teach your kids that whatever they do, work or play, they should put all their energy into it. If they are playing, play hard. If they are studying, study hard. If they are laughing, laugh hard. Live life to the brim. It's a lesson they'll learn from you long before they earn their first paycheck. One of the great qualities of extracurricular activities—drama, music, sports—is that kids learn the value, the joy, and the rewards of hard work. It is, however, up to you to keep the values, joys, and rewards balanced, and to be sure your children are pursuing their goals, not yours.

Third, let your kids experience the joys of work, like overcoming obstacles and enjoying the "I did that" of a finished project, by including them in work around the house. Kids are usually delighted to help, and they love praise for doing their part. Help children and explain things if they need help, but don't do their homework for them because they don't learn that way. And they don't get the self-satisfaction, sense of achievement, and sense of responsibility of having done a task themselves. Nothing gives our children more self-confidence than achieving a goal, and enjoying the fulfillment of completing a task— and then being praised for it.

Many affluent families possess sufficient wealth to ensure that their children can live a comfortable lifestyle without ever doing anything productive in order to pay the rent. These children need to experience the inner satisfaction of achievement so that this natural high is its own reward, and productivity will continue, regardless of the dollars available. For this reason, allowing kids to experience delayed gratification becomes vitally important. When the "I want" demand sounds, parents should insist that the child add this demand to a future wish list visited only on special occasions like birthdays and holidays. "No" is an appropriate word in the parenting vocabulary.

Help your kids understand the difference between needs and wants. So many Americans spend beyond their means because of things they want. We tell our kids that it's okay to want things, but they also need certain things, which is like the difference between school supplies and a new video game. You *need* one and *want* the other.

This is a particularly difficult challenge for people who want to provide their children with things and experiences they didn't have. It is a wonderfully powerful feeling to be able to indulge your kids, but it may be detrimental to them, with the fine line between providing for and spoiling.

When we immediately indulge our kids' continually changing demands, we're doing them an incredible disservice. Spoiled kids never learn how to delay gratification or appreciate the things that they have. They become seriously infected with the disease of entitlement, the misguided belief that privilege is our birthright. Some level of frustration remains a necessary ingredient for achievement. The overindulged child does not tolerate the discomfort of not being instantly gratified and, therefore, will not stick with a task long enough to develop mastery, and to experience the pride and pleasure of achievement. When the going gets tough, they go.

The primary way you avoid creating disincentives for children by giving them too much is to help them develop a sense of self-esteem rooted in reality, and in your love for them. How do you do that? You begin by providing your children with realistic and reasonable expectations. Then you cultivate competency. And you always communicate effectively.

A child develops a sense of accomplishment if expectations are realistic. Sometimes people who are very successful financially place high and even unreasonable expectations on their children. They're used to demanding a lot from themselves, their coworkers, or employees. It can be especially difficult for highly motivated people not to succumb to the belief that they can push and pressure their kids to achieve the levels of performance that they desire for them. Because kids naturally want to please their parents, when they fall short of expectations, it diminishes their sense of being loved unconditionally, and impedes the development of self-esteem.

Naturally, we all have high expectations for our kids, and that in itself is not harmful as long as our expectations are reasonable—and based on the children's abilities, learning styles, and personalities.

Motivation is a self-regulated drive that occurs when the child's activity creates a positive feeling. Children avoid situations that cause stress, frustration, or disappointment. One area in which unrealistic expectations frequently create difficulty is school. Especially if we were good students, we want to see our kids succeed with good grades. However, not every child can be a straight A student. The love of learning is one of the critical life skills that enable each person to achieve his or her own potential, and succeed in the long term. Accordingly, we as parents should stress academic responsibility, and the love of learning as a motivator, rather than grades. Some kids can work really hard with lots of effort and not achieve, and other kids can put in little effort and get A's. Do we agree that the kids who have to work for what they get, as opposed to those who are able to coast, will have more long-term success?

Kids acquire competence through the experience of independently dealing with tasks. However, people who are financially successful are often very self-assertive. Sometimes powerful parents will involve themselves excessively in all aspects of their kids' lives. Operating on the misguided belief that they can prevent their kids from experiencing frustration or disappointment, they continually make important decisions for them. This approach to parenting breeds passive, dependent children who often grow up unable to function independently.

A young child naturally tries to accomplish tasks alone (and should be limited only for issues of safety). But too many parents give too much help. Sometimes I have been guilty of too quickly jumping in if my kids struggle with something. One way to control the natural desire to assist is to stop and ask, "Could my kid perform this task, or any part of it, independently?" If so, let him or her do it. This begins early on with self-care: brushing your teeth, washing your hair, taking a shower, getting dressed, and so forth. And then it progresses to problem solving, dealing with homework, handling interactions with schoolmates, and giving their opinion on a variety of issues.

When the time comes, it is very positive for kids to get summer or after-school jobs. Yes, they do have their whole lives to work, but they have such a great sense of accomplishment when they earn their first money. They also learn to interact in a workplace with coworkers and the boss in quite a different way than they interact with you.

It is also positive to encourage entrepreneurship in kids. To help kids earn money beyond their weekly allowance, you might want to suggest that they find creative ways to make money. The focus should be on "creative" rather than "money." We compensated our kids for doing special chores above and beyond the usual responsibilities, like raking, mowing, watching a neighbor's pet, or babysitting.

Teaching kids the joy of accomplishment, just like teaching values, is a continuous process. Neither can be learned in a fifteen-minute lecture–they take years.

While those teaching tasks are ongoing, a third rule comes into play as your children begin to understand the concept of money and some basic arithmetic.

Rule #3: Let Your Children Manage Money

Kids learn about personal finance and the value of a dollar by doing things for themselves and spending their money on what they want. The choice between a new trinket or baseball now, and a coveted doll or game later, effectively teaches kids to balance short-and long-term desires.

Your child can learn early that saving for something he or she really wants is worthwhile.

Experience teaches that not all things, like toys or treats, are as good as they look on television ads. That's one reason it's good for kids to have some discretionary money. And if it's discretionary, that means you can't veto how your kids spend it. You may want to point out the advantages or disadvantages of spending money a certain way, but if it's their money, let them make the final choice. You may have to grit your teeth as they buy some cheaply made item that you know will soon be gathering dust. But it's one way that they learn the value of wise buying decisions. If they spend their money, and then want something else so badly it tugs at your heartstrings, remind them that IF they hadn't recently spent their money, they could now buy this newest "must-have" item.

It's important to reinforce the value and consequences of both spending and saving decisions, but it's probably wisest to do it as a statement of fact. Don't make children feel stupid for buying something you didn't want them to, even if, in fact, it seemed stupid to you. Rather, make sure that they understand they made a choice–and now have to live with it.

For most of us, our financial lives require constant "either-or" decisions. If you don't face those decisions daily, you either have more money than you can keep track of, are very deep in debt, or are a candidate for sainthood. Kids can learn to address the "either-or" spending and saving dilemma with your gentle guidance. It's a lesson that applies to money—and to most other areas of our lives.

It comes down to valuing our resources,
whether that means money, time, or even trust.
Actions always have consequences.

Allowances

Money management begins with an allowance. There's a lot of debate about the appropriate age to start receiving an allowance. By first grade, age six, most kids can appreciate that money buys things, so that's when we started our two children.

We gave our kids a weekly allowance, to be used however they wanted. It was not a paycheck, paying them to be a part of our household, and doing their share in maintaining our home or their rooms. We expected that without pay. Rather, we gave them an allowance so that they could learn about money and have some measure of independent decision-making–something they control. Restricting an allowance should not be a punishment for inappropriate behavior. In effect, it's really Mom and Dad's money, well spent to teach our kids about money and independence.

Soon after you start your child on an allowance, open a savings account in the child's name because it encourages your child to make saving a habit. Let your child know how much money he or she has.

Some parents feel that they don't have to pay allowances because they generously hand out money whenever their kids want it. But studies have shown that kids who got money from their parents whenever they wanted it tended to save less and were broke more often than kids who received allowances and learned to budget. Even when the total amount of money each group received was the same, the allowance and the responsibility that goes along with it taught kids the value of a dollar for later in life.

Don't just hand out money to your kids whenever they think they want it.

We split our kids' allowances into thirds.

1. One-third could be used for anything they wanted in the short term that they bought with their own money.

2. The second third was for bigger purchases, something that took some time to save for, like a new bicycle. Both my kids used this part to buy presents for each other, making me so proud.

3. The third component went into long-term savings. We periodically emptied the piggybank and deposited the

money into a savings account at a local bank. When their long-term account reached a certain level, we invested the money in mutual funds.

On numerous occasions, we saw that our children understood the lesson we were teaching.

Many parents divide allowances even further so that a portion is set aside for giving to a faith community or charity. This can be an effective way to teach kids to share their good fortune, and to reflect that others' lives may not be as good. Perhaps by doing so, they will appreciate more what they have. If you intend to do this with your child's allowance, allow them some choice and options for which charity gets their money. Doing some research together is another good learning experience.

One of my partners had used an excellent money-management teaching tool with his daughter when she was a high school senior. It worked this way: She deposited her earnings into a debit card account he opened for her, and each month her parents augmented it with an allowance. She started the month with a set amount in her account from her parents, in addition to her earnings. That was all she received. When she needed to buy something, she used her debit card. Because it wasn't a credit card, she could withdraw only what was in the account, and when her account reached zero, she couldn't use her card.

The first month she had the account she used up her money in a week. Of course, she asked her parents for more. They had decided she needed to learn to live on what she had. She figured out how to handle a budget and spend her money carefully, not frivolously. We liked this idea so much that when our children were old enough, we used the same idea.

As your kids go to college, you may want to try another tactic that helps them learn to manage money on a larger scale. If you are blessed with the wherewithal to pay for your kids' college, instead of paying tuition directly to the university from your account, deposit the money into your child's checking account, requiring him or her to write the check.

Writing a check for five figures tells them that their education is important business and gives them a sense of responsibility to take education seriously. It also encourages them to try to do well in college.

How Would You Like to Get Paid?

Once your kids are old enough to understand a bit about money, go through this exercise with them to help them think about saving, as well as earning money with their money. Ask them which way they would prefer to get paid if they were given a job for one month. They could either take $100 a day for their work, or they could get paid one penny the first day and their employer would double their pay every day for thirty days. If they accepted the $100 a day, they could earn $3,000. What could they earn if they accepted a penny the first day, and the amount doubled every day? They would end up with total pay of more than $10 million!

1. $ .01	11. $10.24	21. $10,485.76
2. $ .02	12. $20.48	22. $20,971.52
3. $ .04	13. $40.96	23. $41,934.04
4. $ .08	14. $81.92	24. $83,886.08
5. $ .16	15. $163.84	25. $167,772.16
6. $ .32	16. $327.68	26. $335,544.32
7. $ .64	17. $655.36	27. $671,088.64
8. $1.28	18. $1,310.72	28. $1,342,177.28
9. $2.56	19. $2,621.44	29. $2,684,354.56
10. $5.12	20. $5,242.88	30. $5,368,709.12

Total: $10,737,418.24

Of course, in the real world, money doesn't double that fast. But this exercise is a good introduction for children to the concept of earning some kind of return on their money by saving it, and then investing it.

Have your children write down what they want to do with their money. Writing down goals or plans has a unique impact on our subconscious. Once we see something in writing, it becomes more concrete. It also forces decisions. It's part of the "either-or" process mentioned earlier. Seeing in black and white that we can have one or the other, this or that, focuses attention and energy. With kids, for whom the future often means two hours from now, it helps them understand some of their options with money and life. It's so important, at any age, to have goals in writing that I ask all my new clients to write theirs.

Putting ideas on paper makes them more real. Writing them down forces us to be precise and succinct, to sift through "it would be nice" to get to "this is the most important thing."

We use goal setting with our kids in all aspects of their lives, not just saving and spending. We ask them to think of what big thing that they want to do this year, this month, or the next few years.

Get kids interested in money early. Money is a great way to get kids interested in arithmetic. When they were as young as three or four, we showed our kids how to tell different coins apart. Every day I brought my change home, we counted it and split it evenly between the kids, according to the number of each type of coin, and they put it in their piggy banks. Very quickly both of my kids learned that if they had four quarters or ten dimes that was one dollar. They learned to do the math, and knew in their heads roughly how much money they had.

Keep discussions of money in the family. My kids know that many other kids do not have the same things—and money—they have. Having some money saved is not something to brag about to friends. Whether you and your kids have money or not is simply a fact of their lives. It has nothing to do with character, it has nothing to do with friendships, and it has nothing to do with the people they are becoming. It is a tool that should be respected and valued.

Stress to your kids that our discussions of money are to remain in the family. How much money they have, or even the cost of something they have, is not a proper subject to discuss with their friends or others. Keep discussions of money very general, too, especially in terms of income.

Kids don't need to know how much money you make. Younger children don't have any relative concept of numbers. To them, $100 isn't much different from $100,000. All they need to know about your family's income is that it's enough to buy what your family needs, and perhaps an occasional treat or gift. Especially if money is tight in your family and your kids hear you discussing paying bills or saving and investing, they need reassurance that you have enough money to provide for them.

Money worries should not be a part of your children's lives. As minor as their worries may seem to you, they already worry about a lot. Don't let them think that your family is in any danger or facing hardship.

Lessons I Want My Children to Learn

Lesson #1: Life is not fair, get used to it. One of my daughter's favorite expressions is "That's not fair." My response? "Life's not fair. Who said it was? Get used to it." Depending on the circumstances, of course, I may elaborate. I don't want the phrase to become a cliché, or have her resent or ignore it, so we'll talk about what is fair and how we can make something fairer or more reasonable. But the bottom line is that life often isn't fair.

Lesson #2: The world doesn't care about you. The world expects you to accomplish something before it cares about you. I stress that I always care about them, but they shouldn't expect the same from others.

Lesson #3: No honest job is beneath your dignity. Dignity is a personal, internal characteristic. Doing a job, any job, well is an expression of our personal dignity. Flipping burgers or delivering pizza is not beneath your dignity. I delivered pizzas right after I got married. I did whatever I could to make ends meet and to pay the rent. Some people would call it opportunity.

Lesson #4: If you goof up, it's not someone else's fault. Don't whine about your mistakes, learn from them. The quickest way to end criticism for a mistake, and begin to repair any damage, is to own up to it.

Lesson #5: TV is not real life. In real life, people actually leave the bar or coffee shop and go to work.

Teaching Generosity

My wife was a leader for our daughter's Girl Scout troop, and during the holiday season they held a fundraiser. Their profits were lower than in previous years for a variety of reasons. In the past, the troop had always given a significant amount of the money they raised to buy toys for Toys for Tots around Christmastime, with the remainder of the money going to troop functions and a pizza party. Because the profits were down this year, the girls were reluctant to give money to charity as they had in the past. My wife encouraged them to still give money to charity even though the troop would have less for itself than in previous years. "You get back what you give," she told them.

To the girls' credit, they talked about it, and decided my wife was right. So they donated $25 of their $75 profit to Toys for Tots. A couple of days after this decision, the troop was out caroling for the holiday season, and a local merchant was so impressed by their voices that he asked them to stay on in his store. His customers apparently enjoyed the carols, too. Before the girls finally left, he made out a check as a donation to the troop. The amount? The same $25 the girls had donated to a worthy cause. Of course, my wife did not waste the opportunity to share this lesson with the girls. They had been generous, and had gotten back what they had given. She added, naturally, that the exchange is usually not so immediate and precise.

I firmly believe that when you do well for others, you are rewarded in return, and I've seen it throughout my career. Generosity is an essential piece of glue that holds our culture and society together. You may not always get back exactly what you give, but what we give individually comes back to us as a happier commonwealth.

Beware of the Love of Money

Money is an important tool that our children need to understand, and yet financial literacy is not taught in school. Compound that lack of education with our society's confusing messages about wealth—from images of conspicuous consumption on TV and in movies—and you are left with the difficult job of teaching your children to appreciate, yet not worship, money.

Most kids, except the richest and poorest, grow into their teen years assuming their financial circumstances are the norm. Their own life is all they know, and few of them know others who have either more or less than they have.

What matters most when addressing the issue of money with your children is not how much you or they have. Teach them your values, of which money is a small part, and let them learn to enjoy giving their full energy to whatever they do.

Financier

The "financier" stage of our relationship with our children really begins for most of us when they finish high school and go to college. College tuition is probably the first child-related expense that will require advance planning, investing, or borrowing.

In the past twenty-five years, the escalating costs of higher education have been staggering, matched only by the increases in the cost for medical care. Paying for college has always been an important consideration for parents, but with increases in tuition far higher than the general inflation rate, it has now become a serious planning issue for many families.

Saving for College

Often we know we should be saving for the children's education, but don't act upon that goal. After your home, your child's college education will probably be the second-largest investment or purchase you make in your life.

First among the reasons to save for your child's education is the breathtaking increase in the cost of postsecondary education. In recent years, college costs have increased at a rate far greater than the general rate of inflation. As of this writing, the cost of a college education can vary greatly depending upon whether you're going to a public or private institution. In 2011, the average cost of a state institution ranges from $15,000 to $18,000 per year, and that's if you're an in-state resident. These annual costs included tuition, fees, books, and room and board. Supplies, transportation, and other personal expenses would be additional.

At private institutions, the average was far higher. If you look at universities like Yale, Northwestern, and Stanford, you can expect between $45,000 and $55,000 a year. Assuming an increase of 4 percent per year, by 2016, we will see public institutions cost in excess of $21,000 per year, and private colleges around $52,000 a year. Clearly, the cost of an education is profound, and needs to be planned for properly if it's a priority for you as a parent to pay for your kids' college—or at least assist them with education costs.

Perhaps the most effective way of comparing the increases in college costs is to look at the amount a young person can contribute to the cost of college by working. When I went to college in the 1970s, with a good summer job I could almost pay a year's tuition. A year of college at private institutions now takes almost the median income for a family of four in the United States. Young people are far less likely today to be able to pay even a substantial portion of their tuition by their own labors. Most will need considerable financial assistance.

The second important reason why kids need more help today to pay for education is the years they will probably spend studying before they move into the world of work and paychecks. Many careers now require more than four years of college. Call it degree inflation. Employers in many professions that once required only a bachelor's degree now insist upon, or at least prefer, a master's degree. Moreover, many students today take more than four years to earn their under-graduate degrees.

Is it worth the effort to save and invest to assist your child with college costs? I believe it is.

1. First, let's look at your child's future earning power.

   - According to the U.S. Census Bureau, Educational Attainment, those with a four-year college degree earn an average income of $56,613 while those with only a high school diploma earn an average of $31,283—an annual difference of $25,330.

   - If you multiply that by the estimated years that one will work as an adult, the potential lifetime difference is more than $1.1 million.

2. College also provides young people the opportunity to sample many subjects and discover their true "calling." The discovery and pursuit of that "passion" are perhaps the most important aspect of one's life—even in purely financial terms. Financial success is the result of pursuing

a passion, not money. Not all people who are passionate about what they do are wealthy in financial terms (though many lead rich lives), but very few people become wealthy if they have no passion for what they do.

3. The college experience broadens the horizon of most young people both socially and intellectually. They expand their contacts and friendships beyond what most have in high school. Most of us learned lessons in college that have served us well for many years since. College is a learning experience that little else can equal: how to budget time, how to solve problems, how to think, how to take responsibility for our actions. It is a critical transition into the adult world, as well as the professional world.

4. Young people can emerge from college with new critical thinking skills and an awareness of the world. And it is only the most exceptional people who learn those lessons without the benefit of postsecondary education.

Planning for College Costs

Saving and investing for college is just like any other investment activity: Time is your greatest ally. The sooner you start, the less you have to invest. It may seem a distant goal when your child isn't even in kindergarten yet, but saving for college is much easier if you begin early. Don't wait to start budgeting for it when they begin looking at college brochures.

Step #1: Estimate What College Will Cost When Your Child Is Ready to Go

A financial advisor can help you with this projection. You can also find Internet sites where you can calculate college costs. Factor in things such as the current cost for a year of school, the number of years until your child will begin college, how many years you think it will take him or her to get through college, and an estimated rate of inflation of college costs. Once the total cost is known, you can calculate the amount of monthly or annual savings required to meet that goal.

Step #2: Compare Available Cash Flow with the Savings Required

You need to determine how much financial help you may realistically provide to defray your children's college costs. Paying for four years of college for your kids may not be within the realm of possibility, which is true for many Americans. One client said she had saved enough to pay for two years of college for her daughter, and was wondering about her options for financing the last two years. First I congratulated her on saving as much as she had. Paying for two years of college probably entailed considerable forethought and frugality, and was a wonderful gift to her child. The same may be true for you. Perhaps your child will have to borrow money or work part-time to pay for the rest. That's not all bad.

The key is deciding what you can spare from your weekly, monthly, or yearly budget to contribute to a college fund, and begin to put that money away as soon as you can. The preceding hypothetical example shows that you don't have to contribute thousands a year to pay for four years of college. If you can save something, it will help your child enormously. It's better to save what you can, rather than throw up your hands in frustration at the impossibility of paying for all college costs. If your children are still very young, you may be surprised to find out what you may be able to accumulate in a college fund before they reach college age. Be sure to include in your projections any funds the family may have already saved.

Step #3: Determine and Be Realistic About What Financial Aid May Be Available

Don't count on athletic scholarships. Kids are better off studying than playing sports, because far more financial aid is awarded to good students than to good athletes. A tiny fraction of kids have the physical skills to earn an athletic scholarship, yet playgrounds are full of parents pushing their kids to excel in the unrealistic hope that they might earn one.

When colleges determine eligibility for financial aid, they look at savings in your child's name, but they won't consider some investments in the parent's name, if structured properly. An example is the cash value of life insurance. Money in retirement plans is usually also excluded.

Step #4: Decide How to Invest the Money

Many financial advisors will recommend that money saved for college should be placed in relatively low-risk investments. If you have a long enough time frame, I recommend a more aggressive approach where you initially put your savings in higher-risk or growth types of investments. As the time for college gets closer, the accumulated funds can be shifted from growthoriented assets into more conservative choices, such as fixed-income assets. We typically recommend that for an infant, the investments be made primarily in equities. However, if you are just starting to save for expenses that are only three years away, you might stick with fixed-interest investments.

The ultimate decision depends on a range of factors, such as the number of years until college begins, the amount of money available to invest, and the family's tax bracket, risk tolerance, and investment experience.

Regardless of how you save or where you put the money, the key to successfully saving for your children's college education is to begin as early as possible. Seek professional advice and together, develop a plan to save for college education.

Education Savings Plans in Detail

A number of tax-advantaged strategies are available to accumulate funds for college expenses. Review these complicated rules and strategies carefully with a financial advisor.

The Section 529 Plan

Section 529 Qualified Tuition Plans (QTPs) are one of the most efficient ways of saving for a child's college education. They were established under the provisions of Internal Revenue Code Section 529. They provide a tax-favored framework that funds may be accumulated within to pay for a beneficiary's qualified higher education expenses at an eligible educational institution. You can get a tax advantage if the money is ultimately spent for post-high school education. QTPs allow you either to prepay a student's tuition or to contribute to a savings account established to pay the student's qualified higher education expenses. Both prepaid tuition plans and savings account plans may be established by all of the fifty states. Eligible private institutions are also authorized to establish prepaid tuition plans.

One type of QTP is a prepaid tuition plan. Contributions are made to a qualified trust, which invests the funds to offset increases in tuition costs between now and when the child attends college. The contract allows one to purchase a number of course units or academic periods that are redeemed when the beneficiary becomes old enough to attend college.

In a second type of QTP, a higher education savings account plan, contributions are made to an account established for a named beneficiary. A mutual fund typically manages the investments. The amount available to pay higher education expenses depends upon the growth in the account during the period between which the contribution is made, and when you are ready to make withdrawals for college. Contributions to these programs are not tax deductible; however, the earnings in these accounts grow tax-deferred. If the funds are used for qualified education expenses, earnings are taxed at the beneficiary's tax rate when withdrawn.

Contributions to a QTP must be in cash, and may not exceed the amount necessary to provide the beneficiary's qualified higher education expenses. Program sponsors will specify maximum total contribution amounts based on factors such as the beneficiary's current age, current education costs, projected inflation, and anticipated investment returns. In some programs, up to as much as $240,000 may be contributed for a beneficiary.

Eligibility

Generally speaking, qualified higher education expenses include tuition, fees, books, supplies, and equipment required for attendance. Room and board is also included if the student is attending school at least half-time. Qualified higher education expenses also include costs incurred to allow a special-needs beneficiary to enroll at and attend an eligible institution.

In general, accredited post–high school educational institutions offering associate, bachelor's, graduate level, or professional degrees are eligible. Certain vocational schools are also included.

The beneficiary must be identified at the time the account is created. As a general rule, the person who contributes to the account is the owner. The account owner may change the beneficiary. If the new beneficiary is a member of the same family as the original beneficiary, there's generally no current federal income tax. Qualifying family members include the beneficiary's spouse, son, or daughter, a son or daughter's descendants, stepson or stepdaughter, brother, sister, stepbrother or stepsister, father or mother or ancestor of either, stepfather or stepmother, son or daughter of a brother or sister, brother or sister of a father or a mother, spouse of any person listed above, and first cousins.

More than fifty different 529 plans are available, one for every state. A change in investment strategy is typically permitted at least once each year, or if a new beneficiary is named. Amounts accumulating in a QTP operated by one state generally may be used at educational institutions in a different state. In fact, you could reside in one state, and your beneficiary could reside in the same or a different state as you. You could take the 529 plan from one state, and attend school in yet another state.

Distributions and Taxes

For federal and state tax purposes, funds in a QTP are normally not included in the donor's estate. However, any amounts in a QTP when a beneficiary dies will generally be included in the beneficiary's estate. In other words, if grandparents want to assist a grandchild with college education, and they make a gift to the 529 QTP, they not only get a tax advantage for the beneficiary or the grandchild, they also effectively remove some dollars from their estate.

Qualified Tuition Plan can be an efficient estate-planning tool because it removes assets from the estate.

Another thing to consider with a QTP is that these assets may affect the student's eligibility for financial aid. The U.S. Department of Education has advised that assets in a savings account plan are considered assets of the parent for the purposes of the Free Application for Federal Student Aid (FAFSA). The assets in a prepaid tuition plan are generally considered to reduce the student's need on a dollar-for-dollar basis. Private institutions may also take QTP assets into account when considering financial aid.

In my opinion, the Section 529 Qualified Tuition Plan offers the best benefits if you know your child will ultimately attend higher learning. It is the most efficient due to the tax advantages if the distributions qualify as higher education expenses. However, like everything else with financial planning, flexibility is important, and QTPs are not very flexible apart from the fact that you can change the beneficiary within your family.

If the funds are not used for higher education, the earnings are taxed—either at the owner's tax rate or the beneficiary's tax rate, plus a 10 percent penalty. Regardless of the tax rate, there will always be an additional 10 percent penalty if the funds are not used for higher education. Generally, the QTP owner's tax rate will be higher than the beneficiary's, but not always, so it is worthwhile to double-check.

Coverdell Education Savings Accounts

Another excellent choice for saving for your kids' college education is the Coverdell Education Savings Account. Since 1998, the Coverdell Education Savings Account has offered tax-free withdrawals for higher education. The annual contribution limit is now $2,000 per year. Coverdell accounts, unlike 529 Qualified Tuition Plans, can now be used for elementary and secondary education, and even academic tutoring and education-related computer expenses.

Not everyone is eligible to establish these accounts. If your income exceeds certain limits, you will not be eligible to fund a Coverdell account. Additionally, because annual contributions are limited to $2,000, it can be difficult to accumulate a large amount of money unless you start very early. If you do qualify, the payoff for investing in Coverdell accounts could be substantial. For example, if you contribute $2,000 each year from your child's first year to his or her eighteenth birthday, you could earn a hypothetical 8 percent per year on your investment, and the account would grow to more than $80,000, which should at least make a serious dent in the total cost of four years of college.

Custodial Accounts

The Uniform Gift to Minor (UGMA) or Uniform Transfer to Minor Act (UTMA), which are custodial accounts in the child's name, are less attractive today. For many years, these accounts were the only substantial savings vehicle for education expenses. As a result, many people have built up sizable amounts in custodial accounts. Unlike Coverdell accounts, there are no income or contribution limits. At least part of the earnings on the investment may be exempt from

Federal income tax, or some or all are taxed at the child's lower rate if the child is under the age of 24.

Money can be withdrawn at any time for the benefit of the child—not only for education—with certain limitations. Contributions to UGMAs and UTMAs are irrevocable, meaning that once the money or other property is put in, the donor cannot change his or her mind and withdraw the gift. No doubt the major drawback to custodial accounts is that the child assumes control of the account upon reaching the age of majority, which is 18 or 21 in most states.

I prefer to see education savings remain in the parents' or grandparents' names. If the custodial account is in your son's name, he could spend it on a new car instead of college once he reaches age 18 or 21. If it's in your name, the decision is yours. The tax benefits of accounts in a child's name are relatively small, and not an important factor. Moreover, money in the child's name is usually considered when determining financial aid, whereas money held by the parents in some accounts may not be counted in calculating need-based financial aid.

Borrowing Money for Education

As I wrote in Chapter 1, in the section on debt, I believe borrowing for education is one of the only good uses of debt. Student loans typically charge very low interest rates, are amortized over a long period of time, and are used to buy an appreciating asset. A college degree, on average, leads to higher lifetime earnings, thus a good investment.

Does it make sense to borrow from a 401(k) or other pretax retirement account to pay for college? In my opinion, it does *not* make sense, and I would recommend against this risk, unless there is no alternative.

Borrowing against retirement savings should be a last resort for paying college costs.

One reason is that you could face severe penalties if you had a financial emergency that caused you to miss payments on loans against your pretax retirement account. The IRS would then treat the entire amount you borrowed, even amounts already repaid, as an early withdrawal. You'd have to pay penalties and income taxes on all of it.

Instead of borrowing against your retirement account, one option is to not contribute to your 401(k) for a couple of years, putting that money toward college costs.

If you do need to borrow money for college beyond student loans, borrow against any equity in your home before you borrow from your retirement.

Too few people consider the option of permanent life insurance. It can be an excellent way to save for college for parents who are somewhat young and healthy, so the cost of the death benefit is relatively low. Most policies allow borrowing against the cash value of the policy at attractive interest rates. Another advantage of investing with permanent life insurance is that most colleges don't consider the cash value of life insurance when determining eligibility for financial aid. Moreover, there are no limits on the amount that can be invested each year, unlike IRAs and most 401(k)s. For a detailed discussion of permanent life insurance, refer to Chapter 5.

Benefactor

Each of us leaves a legacy to our children. Producing your own personal legacy is an art form, like writing a symphony. And like the composition of a symphony, your wealth management solutions will require thought, planning, and creativity. Estate planning is about living. What you do with your estate is not just a matter of death and dying. How you plan the distribution of your assets helps define who you are, how you think of yourself, your aspirations, and your sense of purpose in life.

- Who will benefit from your life's work?

- Will it be the people you want to benefit?

- How can you be sure they will receive what you want them to receive when you're gone?

Your estate plan helps answer these questions. If you haven't created an estate plan, you may be surprised to know you actually already have one–by default, imposed by the probate and tax laws of the state of your residence. But this plan does not necessarily ensure that your assets are given to the people you love.

The purpose of your estate plan is to distribute the property you've accumulated over a lifetime exactly as you wish. Your goals may include ensuring that you have a solid retirement program, providing for your surviving family members, or supporting the work of charitable causes. Your concerns may include determining who needs or deserves your gifts most, whether your gifts will be used prudently, and how to reduce losses from taxes.

For example, it's possible to set up a trust for your heirs, which contributes to your peace of mind and expresses your love and concern. It's also possible to donate property to charities while retaining lifetime ownership and use.

When working with the right financial services team, and taking into account your personal vision, estate planning can be one of the most fulfilling projects you will ever undertake.

Life Versus Legacy

On your role as benefactor to your children, here are two important points:

1. Your legacy to your children can't make up for your failures as a provider, protector, or teacher. Your children will probably get along just fine without your money after you die. They won't do nearly so well if they don't get

your time, your values, and your love while you're alive. Your first and most important legacy to your children is the way you lived, and your relationships with them. Money will not mend fences that were broken long ago. If amends need to be made, don't rely on your estate to do it after you're gone.

2. Consider the impact of your estate and your will on those you leave behind. Wills can leave bitterness among family members when assets are bequeathed inequitably. Will your estate unite or divide your family? Leaving an estate to your children should be your last act of love for them, not a parting shot in a long-running argument. If you have good reason to divide your estate in certain ways— perhaps one child provided care for you in your later years—you can always take the time, and then summon the words, to express your wishes and your reasons if you have chosen not to divide your estate equally among your children.

Estate planning isn't always easy, and some people feel overwhelmed and not comfortable talking about the things that make it difficult: our fears, our hopes, and family conflicts. Many people find it difficult to think about dying, and about how things might be when they are gone. For some, estate planning can be an isolating experience, especially when family situations arise that can't be resolved easily. Treating death as an intensely private topic–to be avoided at all costs–takes an emotional and spiritual toll on all parties.

Creating your estate plan, knowing that you have found a smart way to pay estate taxes, enrich the lives of those you love, or support the causes that mean the most to you, can be an opportunity to break the silence and to better understand the rich fabric of family and social relationships that make up your life.

Money and Your Children's Children

The relationship between grandparents and their grandchildren is unique, and can be loving and rewarding for all. This special relationship often results in grandparents wanting to assist their grandchildren financially.

That desire is admirable. Even more admirable is a willingness to give them your time and love. Babysit your grandkids. Play catch. Teach them to fish, to golf, to play a musical instrument. Take them to the theater. Give them your time and love, and chances are they'll make you proud and use your financial gifts to better themselves, and thus make gift giving more rewarding for you.

As your grandchildren grow up, don't overlook the benefit to them of your experience. You may be able to give them advice or help them with problems that they may not be as willing to address with their parents. You will probably have few chances in life to be as revered as a role model as you are with your grandchildren.

Grandparents have the unique prerogative to spoil their grandchildren—with one caveat. Include your children in any discussion of how to assist your grandchildren, financially or otherwise. Despite your love for your grandchildren, you still have a "grand" in front of your name. You are not the parents, and should not make decisions without their input.

Loving grandparents who want to help financially can do a lot. But some things cannot be done legally, or are inadvisable. Let's consider some of the possibilities.

Gifts

Cash gifts of up to $13,000 per year can be given to a grandchild without gift tax consequences for the child. I would caution you to understand the consequences of putting large sums of money in an account in a young child's name, because then you have no control over how it is spent.

IRA

When a grandchild can legitimately earn income and receive a W-2 or 1099, the grandparent may contribute to an IRA or Roth IRA in the grandchild's name, limited to earned income, up to $5,000 annually. *You may not open an IRA or Roth IRA in the name of a child who does not have earned income.* One must have earned income in order to contribute to an IRA or Roth IRA. Employing the child in a family business or to assist you is a legitimate way for the child to earn income toward the $5,000 threshold, as long as actual work is done, and is compensated at realistic rates of pay.

Real Estate

Too often, a grandparent wants to put a grandchild's name on the deed to property to ensure the grandchild receives the property on the death of the grandparent. Don't do this for two reasons. One, by making a grandchild a co-owner, they might have to pay gift tax on a portion of your home's value; two, if you make him co-owner now, it could be more expensive for them if they ever wanted to sell the house. Their basis in the house would be its value when *you* acquired it, which increases the likelihood that the grandchild would pay capital gains taxes. The simplest solution is to designate in your will that you want he or she to have the house. For tax purposes, they would then acquire the house at its value when you die, making it less likely that they would pay capital gains if they sold it.

Education

Helping to pay for post–high school education is a priority for many grandparents. You have several options to help out.

Education IRAs, otherwise commonly known as a Coverdell Education Savings Account

Grandparents can contribute up to $2,000 per year per grandchild with no tax liability for the grandchild, if used for education. (That means Grandma can't contribute any money if Grandpa has already met the $2,000 contribution limit for that year.) One note of caution: $2,000 per year, when started at infancy, is only a total investment of $36,000 ($2,000 x 18 years). Even with excellent investment results, it won't cover college costs for long, given the rate of increase of education expenses. One other note to consider is that the contribution is subject to limits based on the adjusted gross income of the grandparent.

Qualified Tuition Plans (QTPs) or 529 Plans

As described earlier, these college savings plans are state-sponsored investment programs. Anyone can contribute to a QTP for a child, with a maximum contribution of $65,000 per person (5 years of $13,000 gift exclusion in one year without using a lifetime gift exemption). All earnings accumulate tax deferred, and withdrawals for qualified education expenses might be tax-free. These savings plans can be an efficient way to defray education costs, especially for grandchildren who are unlikely to qualify for financial aid. QTPs offer an advantageous way for grandparents in high tax brackets to transfer assets to their grandchildren. Unlike a Coverdell, there are no income limits for allowance of contributions to a QTP.

Transferring Highly Appreciated Assets

Giving highly appreciated assets to a grandchild over age 24, or to their educational institution, can be tax efficient. The alternative of selling the asset, and then making a gift, could cause a huge tax liability to the giver.

Legacy

When they die, many grandparents choose to transfer assets directly to their grandchildren. Doing so can be done efficiently as an act of love, as an investment in your own gene pool, and as a way to shield some of your estate from taxes.

Roth IRA

Name your grandchild the beneficiary of a Roth IRA. When you die, he or she then receives the proceeds income tax–free if distributions don't occur until at least five years after you open the account. While you could also make your grandchild the beneficiary of a regular IRA, the proceeds of that IRA would be subject to income tax for your grandchild. They also don't have to take distributions all at once. Grandchildren can potentially "stretch" the tax benefits of these accounts for up to 82.4 years, depending on their age when they inherit the account. That's a lot of tax benefits. You can only make contributions to a Roth IRA, however, if you still have earned income. If you have earned income of at least $5,000 per year, you can contribute up to $5,000 per year to a Roth. The same is true for your spouse.

Life Insurance

Life insurance can be an extremely effective strategy for transferring assets to grandchildren. The grandparent applying for the insurance should be healthy and able to fund the life insurance for at least ten years for it to be efficient. Distributions and the death benefit may be income tax–free. The life insurance may also be beneficial to the grandparents in their estate planning by creating an infusion of capital that their heirs could use to offset estate tax liability.

Survivorship Insurance

Survivorship life insurance is a form of insurance that provides one policy that insures the lives of two people. It will pay a death benefit only upon the death of the last surviving insured person. Often used by a married couple in estate planning.

Planning helps protect your children financially and helps educate them. But even more important, it takes away the work and worry of money matters so you can spend time with your children. Make no mistake; children are expensive. But they're worth it because they add immeasurably to your life.

There are four stages of the financial relationship you have with your children:

1. **Protector and provider.** It goes beyond the essentials of food, clothing, and shelter to helping them lead happy, productive lives. And then it goes further by ensuring they'll be well cared for should anything happen to you.

2. **Teacher.** It's your job to help your children grow up ambitious, productive, unspoiled, and financially smart. Teaching them how to think about, and behave with, money are essential parts of that job, and you do it by teaching your children values.

3. **Financier.** This stage is primarily about saving, planning, and paying for college. It's important to understand all the options, and their pluses and minuses.

4. **Benefactor.** This is all too easy to do wrong and end up leaving bitterness instead of a legacy of love. Take the time and energy to make an estate plan with professionals.

And if you have grandchildren, there are many financial tools and instruments you can use to help them, while also avoiding or reducing your taxes and theirs.

CHAPTER 3

Mom and Dad and Money

A financial relationship between an adult child and his or her parents has steadily become a more important issue in my business—from the perspective of the adult child. Why have things changed? Because the much longer life expectancy makes this more important, from a financial-planning perspective.

Most likely your parents will live considerably longer than parents did in the past. Many retired people have at least one parent still alive and healthy. Both generations might be senior citizens, often living off fixed incomes, either through pensions or retirement savings. Here's the financial concern: Your parents might need financial assistance from you—and because you are no longer earning an income from your skills or labor, the need increases for preparation and planning before you reach retirement.

The phenomenal rise in medical and health care costs in the past couple of decades also affects the financial relationship between these generations. Some of the medical advances that contribute to greater longevity are very expensive.

This increase in medical costs, which can sap a life's savings in no time, has increased the need for financial planning for parent and child alike.

And the truly staggering sums of money that today's adult children will inherit in the next few years from their parents has also changed the financial relationship. Children are not responsible for planning the passing of wealth from one generation to the next, but they will often be involved in that planning, and they will certainly be required to manage the inheritance when it passes to *them*.

From working with a wide variety of clients, I see three important financial issues involving money and parents, one of which you will likely have to address with your parents or on their behalf. Those three issues are:

1. Caring for elderly parents;

2. Wills and estate planning; and

3. Managing an inheritance.

Communication between parents and children on these issues is often difficult. If you think a family has a hard time talking about finances, bring up the subject of a death in the family. In this chapter, I want you to talk about the two things that many families talk about least—and combine the two in one conversation. Take heart. In most human interaction, you'll be rewarded richly for the energy you expend to understand another person. And you have a huge head start: You love each other.

Caring for Elderly Parents

One of the most difficult jobs you might face in life is caring for a parent, physically or financially. This is not because of the strain it could place on your body, your schedule, or your bank account, but because of the fundamental emotional shift it requires. It's hard to become the parent to the man who tossed you in the air as a child, catching you in his unfailing big hands. And the woman who was your primary source of care and comfort, who was always there with wisdom or just the right touch to perk up your spirits—this shift requires you to accept a world and a relationship that have turned upside down.

Keep in mind as you provide such care that the relationship is as new and difficult for your parent as it is for you. Especially in the United States, where independence, self-reliance, and financial success is so celebrated, too many older people see any kind of dependence on their children as a sign of failure in their own lives. That is unfortunate, because to me, raising children who are sympathetic, empathetic, and willing to give of themselves to others is one of the greatest successes any parent can achieve.

The same attributes that mark a healthy relationship between parent and child from early in their lives together—honest and open communication—are still essential. As an adult child, you have to be willing to talk about the difficult choices you have to make together. If you think you can help, offer. As a parent, you have to be honest about your own fears and worries. If you think you need help, ask. No subjects should be out of bounds for either of you, not long-term illness, not even death. Talking about your futures will make them less frightening for both of you.

Two subjects involving money are perhaps the most worrisome for children as they seek to provide assistance to elderly parents.

1. How are the parents managing their money?

2. Will they be able to afford the longer-term care they may need, sooner or later?

Protecting the Nest Egg

It may sound selfish for children to worry about their parents' assets, but it is not. Many people express concerns to me about their elderly parents' use of money, not because of their desire to inherit it, but because of their increasing protectiveness of their parents.

A friend recently admitted his concern that his eighty-year-old father, a frugal hourly-wage earner his entire working life, was no longer content to have a couple thousand in his checking account. He was starting to maintain balances of $40,000 to $50,000. This uncharacteristic behavior of shifting retirement assets into a liquid account had my friend worried. He had no interest in an inheritance because he was also very successful financially. What bothered him was that his father, who had spent so carefully and saved so religiously during his life, was in danger of blowing his nest egg. Of course, part of his concern was for his mother, who was in better health. But the other part of his concern was for his father's emotional state, and the impact it would have on his father if he were to fall prey to a scam or throw away his hard-earned money some other way.

Some children in this position react in opposite ways. One says it's none of his business; his parents earned the money, saved the money, and can spend it however they wish. The other extreme is to initiate action to seek control over a parent's finances. In most cases, neither extreme is appropriate. A better reaction is to find a way to talk about your concerns in the context of your parents' financial plans: their income and saving, their ability to pay for long-term care, and their estate plans. You might suggest that they seek the advice of a financial professional to assist them, or at least review their plans. Parents sometimes feel more comfortable talking about finances, which they consider family secrets, with a neutral professional.

Most important is your parents' health and happiness. If medical conditions are present, such as Alzheimer's, that may impair your parent's ability to make good decisions, perhaps then you should seek greater involvement in managing their finances. But if that is not the case, if your parents are simply being a bit wasteful with resources they are pretty sure they can't outlive, maybe you should let them have their day.

Elder Care

The second important issue for adult children assisting elderly parents is long-term care, a costly issue both financially and emotionally. The easiest solution for some people would be simply to purchase long-term care insurance. Long-term care insurance, however, is not a feasible option for many. Because of the cost, long-term care insurance is financially most efficient for those who are trying to protect their estate from being spent down.

The reality for some people is that by the time they look into long-term care protection, they have already encountered some type of medical problem that would disqualify them.

By the time most children are involved in their parents' longer-term decisions, the parents are already in crisis-control mode.

Addressing a crisis requires first that we examine all of our options. To pay for nursing home care, hospice, assisted living, or elder care, you have essentially four choices: private pay (meaning the patient pays for it out of pocket), long-term care insurance, Medicare, and Medical Assistance.

If you are indeed facing a crisis, private pay is probably out of the question, and likely so is long-term care insurance. That leaves Medicare and Medical Assistance.

Many people get confused about the difference between Medical Assistance and Medicare. Medicare is an entitlement program much like Social Security. In fact, you make regular contributions to Medicare, just like Social Security, through mandatory deductions from your pay. Medicare covers certain health care costs, and will cover nursing home care costs under certain circumstances. Medical Assistance, on the other hand, is a welfare program. Eligibility is determined by the person's assets. The person must qualify to receive Medical Assistance benefits, and, once eligibility is established,

Medical Assistance will pay for all health care costs. Eligibility is determined by the person's assets. That's the simple explanation. In reality, the criteria for eligibility are complex.

This is where we often turn to an attorney specializing in elder care. Elder-care law is a relatively new term referring to areas of law that affect the elderly, including estate planning, probate, and trust administration. It can also include disability planning, advanced directives, guardianship and conservatorships, and, of course, long-term care planning.

A Plan for Parents

For some, planning for our aging parents' care is a legitimate contingency in our financial plans. Most adult children have at least a vague idea of whether their parents will require financial assistance or guidance from them well before they reach the age when it may become a crisis. But there is only one way to know for sure: Ask. Talk about finances with your parents early enough to get a clearer picture of how their needs may affect your finances and planning. Your questions may be met by silence or diversions, but they may not be. It's a safe bet that your parents think about their financial situation often. Who doesn't? They probably have a pretty good idea of their financial future, and will give you at least a glimpse of it.

For those of you who have adult children, initiate the discussion. Let your kids know if you have worries about your finances or if you have sufficient assets that they should never have to consider assisting you. Tell them whether you have a financial plan. If you find it difficult to discuss your specific finances with your children, at least give them a clue. Just remember how infuriating it was when as teenagers, they never seemed to communicate with you—even on matters that you thought were important. Don't behave like an old teenager with your own children. Talk to them. They probably want to know, but are not sure how to ask, just like you years ago.

Planning Ahead

It's not your money yet, but you can do some things to still help your parents manage their finances—if they allow it.

Wills and estate planning were discussed earlier from a different perspective, but the same issues can also be important from adult children's perspectives as they look to their parents' financial future.

The most important thing you can do is to encourage your parents to have a written, legal will. Present this simple rationale: Don't make us guess what you want us to do with your estate, and don't leave it to the courts or state law.

Laws in your state may divide your parents' estate exactly as they would like. That's fine as long as they are making that choice. But sometimes leaving estates to be decided by law can be grossly unfair.

Chuck, the Dairyman

Growing up in rural Minnesota in the heart of an agricultural county, I knew a lot of farmers.

Chuck, a very successful dairyman and breeder of Holsteins, was always going to get his estate in order and work with me, as he often said: "As soon as they quit screwing around with tax laws, and we know what we're dealing with."

One day his son, Bob, called to say that his dad had died, and he wanted to know if we had done any planning together. I offered my condolences, but told him that Chuck had never done business with me or likely anyone else. Bob was very upset because he thought his dad had planned his estate. Bob was one of eight kids, but the only one to stay on the farm. He thought he was working for his future and would be justly rewarded, but now his seven siblings were all going to share equally in the estate. Chuck's dairy farm was a huge operation.

Unfortunately, it is all gone now. The cows were sold, the real estate was sold, and a huge tax was paid. Bob, who had been a critical component in the growth and the success of the operation, was left with little, and had to start over. He no longer speaks with any of his siblings, who received the same benefits he did from the estate.

Could Bob have done more while his father was alive? Probably, although given that family's culture of silence about family finances (common in that type of community), any efforts by Bob to suggest an equitable division of an estate might have been met with silence from Chuck. Perhaps Bob could have proposed becoming a formal partner in the ownership of the farm or some of its assets, which might have stimulated a productive discussion. The fact that Bob did not know whether his father had made any plans suggests that he was not as aggressive or astute as he could have been in divining his father's plans, and in accumulating some assets in his own name.

The Need to Know

Adult children should know whether their parents have made provisions for their later years–and for their estates. Asking if your parents have made those plans is appropriate. It is not prying. Of course, the parents are free to reveal as many or as few details as they are comfortable doing.

The primary motive in asking should not be to ascertain how much of an inheritance you will receive so that you can plan your purchase of a new lake home. Rather, the point in asking—and you should make this clear—is that you would like to know if assisting your parents at some point is a contingency you should consider in your financial planning. Likely one of your parents will live for some time after the other dies. When your father or mother is alone, his or her needs may change, and he or she is also more likely to rely on you for input and advice on financial plans. It would be helpful for both of you to have some idea of what to expect in the future.

Second, you might have more knowledge of estate planning tools (especially after reading this book), and can suggest some useful options for your parents to consider. If your parents do reveal to you enough of their finances and thoughts on their estate that you know you will inherit some assets, you should bring to their attention any estate-planning options that could be beneficial to both of you.

One of the best ways for you to ensure that your parents' finances in life and death are in the best shape they can be is to encourage them to formalize their plans with a financial advisor. That takes the onus off you to manage their finances, but gives you some assurance that they will receive good advice and learn about new, efficient planning options. They maintain their independence, and you get some peace of mind that their lives will be lived as they wish, and that their financial legacy to their family will be all that it can be.

Living Will/Advance Health Care Directive

Addressing the eventual death of your parents is not easy, but you know it will happen. Discussing estate issues is not morbid; on the contrary, it is very helpful for families to talk about the issues surrounding death or serious illness. Know your parents' wishes about the extent of medical treatment they wish to receive if they suffer serious illness or injury. These wishes are often referred to as a "living will" or "advance health care directive," and are best put in writing. Do your parents want to be resuscitated in a medical emergency? In what circumstances? Would they want to be kept alive by a respirator and feeding tube? They can make their wishes known for such possibilities in an advance health care directive.

Most states have online forms for people to complete on their own. Most states also require witnessing. Anything your parents write by themselves or with a computer software package should follow their state's laws. Your parents should consider asking the same lawyer who drew up their will to also draw up their advance health care directive.

By all means they should discuss their health care desires with their physician. He or she is likely to be the one caring for your parents and is more likely to honor requests that have been communicated directly. Their physician can help them phrase their requests to make sense to medical professionals and can answer any questions. He or she can also point out illogical or inconsistent features of their requests, and tell them if there are aspects that he or she cannot honor for personal, moral, or professional reasons.

It is important for them to discuss their desires with family and friends so they can clarify the directives on the basis of recollections of specific discussions. And if they have discussed their wishes with a number of people, it is more likely that their wishes will be honored.

They should keep the original in an easily found place, and you should know where that is. The person who will execute their wishes (probably you) should get a copy, as should family members and other loved ones, and their doctor. And they should ask that a copy be placed in their medical records.

Although it is not necessary to have it in writing as with a living will, you should also know your parents' wishes for their physical remains. Do they want to be buried? If so, where? Have they made provisions for burial already? Or do they want to be cremated? They may even have clear preferences for the type of funeral or memorial service.

My friend's father, a retired Methodist minister, has given explicit instructions. He wants to be cremated, with no public funeral and no open casket. Rather, he wants a memorial service that would consist mainly of singing joyous Christian hymns such as "How Great Thou Art." Through the grace of his father, my friend does not have to make a lot of difficult decisions at a time of loss and grieving. His father has spared him that by relating exactly what he wants done upon his death.

The issue of living wills is often a nonthreatening opening to talk with your parents about their "other" will and their estate planning. In my opinion, you have an obligation and a right to know your parents' wishes for their lives, their deaths, and their legacies.

In my opinion, you have an obligation and a right to know your parents' wishes for their lives, their deaths, and their legacies.

Inheriting Money

Let's conclude our discussion of money and parents on a positive note. Many people have not considered: What will you do with the money you might inherit from your parents?

We probably all know people who will inherit a few million from their very successful parents. Far more of us will inherit not those large sums, but still substantial assets that could have a significant impact on our own lives and those of our children.

Consider this alarming statistic: In more than 70 percent of inheritances of $100,000 or more, the beneficiaries have completely spent the money in less than two years.

In the coming years we will see the acceleration of an unprecedented transfer of wealth. People often speak of Baby Boomers as the generation that has driven much of our culture and behavior for the past fifty-plus years. While that may be true, what enabled Baby Boomers to be the driving force in our society was the unparalleled economic success of their parents. The "Greatest Generation," to use Tom Brokaw's term, did far more than win World War II. They provided the energy for a period of tremendous prosperity following the war, a period that, one could argue, has continued with only minor hiccups until the present day. That long period of prosperity, combined with the frugality of the generation—many grew up in the Great Depression—led to an accumulation of wealth, even among average working people, that is now being passed down to their children. I'm surprised that we have not seen more research on the topic, more analysis of the historical forces that created it, and more speculation on the impact it will have on our society. Given this enormous transfer of wealth, which some estimates put at more than $10 trillion, many of us will wrestle with what to do with an inheritance, perhaps unexpected in its size.

The First Reaction

Inheriting money, particularly life-changing sums of money, can spark financial and emotional reactions, and possibly problems, for people who have never thought about or prepared for it. Some of the potential difficulties include:

- **Grief.** Inherited money usually comes at a deep personal cost: the death of a loved one. This personal pain may cloud your financial and emotional judgment regarding your inheritance.

- **Guilt.** Experts who work with "inherited wealth" say that guilt is a far more common and more powerful emotion among heirs than people realize. It's often the cause for doing nothing with an inheritance, or even disclaiming it. Heirs often ask themselves what they did to earn the money other than win the gene pool lottery. Some also have philosophical differences with how the money was acquired, maybe considering it "dirty money."

- **Anger.** Anger often complicates the grieving process, as well as making financial decisions. Anger can arise when someone doesn't receive as much money as they thought they would, or thought they deserved. Perhaps they feel there is an inequitable distribution among several heirs, including their siblings. Heirs sometimes measure the benefactor's love by the size of the inheritance. Ironically, some heirs are angry for quite a different reason: They receive well more than they thought they would, but they become angry because they've lived frugally, and could have used the money years earlier.

- **Inadequacy.** Wealth is often created by talented, resourceful, and dynamic people. An heir may feel inadequate or unworthy of the inheritance because he or she doesn't possess the same talents as the benefactor.

- **Paralysis.** People who are not competent or experienced with handling money, commonly those who inherit at a young age or never learn good money management practices, may simply be paralyzed by what to do with inherited money. For example, the deceased may have handled all of the family finances, and now the surviving spouse or child doesn't know what to do, so they do nothing, or they spend it immediately and recklessly, which results in regret or financial hardship later.

- **Conflict with spouse.** Spouses can disagree over what to do with an inheritance, especially if they have conflicting money personalities. The heir may feel it is his or her money, and does not want to share it with the spouse, or the non-heir may feel inadequate because the partner has brought disproportionate wealth into the household.

In each of these cases, time is often a cure. To the extent that you are able, you should try to separate your reaction to a death from decisions that need to be made about an inheritance. Give yourself time to grieve. Some financial issues may need to be addressed soon after a death, but try to defer your big decisions until you have had an appropriate time to grieve.

Avoid making all financial decisions that can be deferred until you are ready to deal with them.

If you are fortunate, other than inheriting a considerable sum of money, your parents will have engaged in some long-range planning before death. They may have established trusts to control their estates, given away some of their money while still alive, or at least explained what you might expect to inherit, and perhaps even why.

Surprise!

What if you inherit money without adequate preparation from the benefactor?

First, do as you would if you were to win the lottery. The key is to think before acting.

Don't do anything for a while, maybe even as much as six months. Put the cash in a money market account; don't sell off any inherited stock right away unless there's a serious risk that it will lose significant value; keep the business or the farm running as usual; and maintain any property. Take time to make sound decisions.

Make a list of what you could do with the inheritance. Let your mind roam freely. You'll probably soon realize how quickly your list eats up all the inheritance. At that point, begin to do some realistic prioritizing. Think about what you can do with this money that matches your own values—values that in most cases were learned from the parent who bequeathed the money. Perhaps you want to donate a portion of it, or put some toward college for your kids. If you have problems with how the money was acquired, consider "cleaning" what you think of as dirty money, by donating it to a charitable cause instead of merely disclaiming it.

Most important, develop a plan for how you will use the money. Incorporate it into your existing financial plan. Even if the sum of inherited money is substantial enough to change the way you might live, it's a good idea to stick to the basic objectives of your earlier plan. If that plan reflects your values and your goals, as it should, new money shouldn't change that. Instead, look at the new money as a way to go further down your list of goals or to strengthen parts of your plan.

Do not let more money, however acquired, change your core values, the way you think you should live your life, and your relationships to the people you love.

Second, seek professional advice. Perhaps you really need the services of a counselor, pastor, or mental health professional to help you come to terms with the inheritance—and your relationship with your benefactor. Then a qualified financial advisor can help you make sound financial decisions. Sadly, heirs are frequently targets for investment schemes and scams. A financial advisor can help you deal with those unscrupulous people. Most important, an advisor can help you create a plan that will make your inheritance an asset in reaching your dreams and goals as well as those of the people you love.

A financial advisor can also help you negotiate the tangled tax laws that address estates and inherited property. Estate tax laws have been the subject of considerable political and legislative debate in both Washington, D.C., and many state capitals. But even without estate taxes to worry about—and the vast majority of people won't have to, regardless of whether estate taxes are repealed—many other potential tax questions arise for those who inherit assets.

- **Example:** A client's father recently died, and the client sold his father's home for $250,000. He received a 1099 form reporting that as income. He wondered if he had to pay income tax on that amount. He did not. He will have to report that 1099 income on Schedule D on his tax return, but he will also be asked his "basis" in the property, the value when he acquired it, to determine whether he realized a gain on the sale. In fact, his basis was the same, $250,000, as the price for which he sold the home. The result was a gain of zero, creating no income tax. In this case, the father's total estate was not subject to estate taxes.

Inheriting Responsibility

Most of us who stand to inherit some money from our parents will get it only when both parents have died. In most cases, one parent's assets will pass to the surviving spouse. Statistically, the first to die is usually the father. That may mean if your father dies first, your mother may want or need help to manage her assets. The money is still hers—her financial situation might not have changed at all with the death of your father—but she now has a new responsibility.

It is not inappropriate to ask your mother if she needs any help or to offer your assistance. Often with clients I've seen that the mother is somewhat more comfortable discussing her finances, even admitting her own sense of incompetence in financial matters, with a financial advisor, rather than with her children. Do not be offended for secrecy regarding family finances, especially among those of a certain age, extends even to their children.

The best assistance you might provide in this case is to help your mother find a competent financial advisor that she can trust. It may be the best protection you can offer her, especially in that most vulnerable time after she has lost her lifelong partner, and is probably overwhelmed by grief and anxiety at the thought of life alone.

Let me repeat: Money is one of many tools that may help you accomplish your objectives in life. When you inherit money, whether a pleasant surprise or anticipated, take the time to put the new resources in their proper place in your life.

An efficient financial plan that makes wise use of your inherited resources is often one of the best ways to honor the person who chose you to be the steward of his or her financial legacy.

CHAPTER 4

Estate Planning Is About Living

Estate planning is simple, yet 50 percent of Americans have none of the most basic estate planning documents in place. Only 35 percent of Americans have a basic will. And only 29 percent of Americans have a current living will (or health care directive). Every day we meet with, and hear from, people who, unfortunately, often through no fault of their own, have misconceptions about what estate planning really means, nor about how important it is to almost everyone. These are some of the things we hear:

- We don't need "estate" planning—we're not the Rockefellers.

- My beneficiary designations might be outdated, but my will is what counts.

- I've got a will. That's my estate plan.

- I'm leaving everything to my spouse—that's the right way to go.

- There's no way to avoid paying taxes on our estate.

- I already have a financial plan, so I don't need an estate plan.

- My family would never argue about their inheritance.

While these are common misconceptions, none of them is correct. Here's a straight-talk definition of estate planning:

Doing the right things to allow you to prosper and protect your assets while you're alive, working with your financial advisors and attorney to ensure that your property goes to the people you love and the causes you care about, and creating a strategy that will minimize your taxes.

As you can see from the definition, estate planning doesn't just cover what happens at a person's death. Your estate plan can help you while you're very much alive and well, protecting your assets now, and providing income while you're healthy and enjoying retirement. Through estate planning tools like life insurance, annuities, and charitable trusts, you can provide for your own needs while ensuring that the bulk of your assets is distributed according to your values and wishes.

During your lifetime, an estate plan allows you to:

- Identify who will make financial and medical decisions if you're ever incapacitated

- Give direction about life-support measures you may or may not want taken in the event of a terminal illness

Upon your death, an estate plan:

- Names guardians for your minor children

- Describes exactly how you'd like your assets distributed

- May enable you to reduce the effect of federal and state estate and gift taxes

- May help your heirs avoid probate court and the lengthy probate process

Your estate is created from savings from your earnings, ownership in businesses, investment growth, and inheritance. Life insurance is often a method of creating an estate for heirs, should one die prematurely. Once the estate is created, life insurance can be structured so that it can be used as a means to offset costs to close out your estate and estate taxes. Then you have to preserve it from income and estate taxes, and from inflation, the biggest forces that erode our estates' value. Careful planning can help us reduce or avoid estate and income taxes, and outrun inflation. And finally, you have to plan how to pass it on, or distribute it.

Where Do You Start?

I approach estate planning a bit differently, almost backward from how it's traditionally done. First I look at a client's income needs for the lifestyle they want, which is driven by their core values, or what is most important to them. Only then do I look at how they can use what remains to create an estate for their children or others. I base estate planning on their excess cash flow, money they don't need and wouldn't spend.

For instance, paying a premium for life insurance in order to give more money to charity or to benefit your children may be generous, but I don't want clients to be saddled with costs, overhead, or premiums that might diminish their lifestyle. A cash-flow analysis ensures that they can live as they want in their later years, which I believe is more important than the size of their estate. After the analysis, I look at buying insurance for estate planning only if they can pay the cost of the insurance without detracting from their lifestyle.

Inventory

To start estate planning, you need:

1. An inventory of all your holdings and their fair market value.

2. A list of all your debts and expenses, including mortgages and other loans.

3. A projection of funeral expenses and estate administrative costs.

Typically, an individual owns property outright. How the property is owned is important because this will control how it passes to your heirs. For example, property held solely in your name or as "a tenant in common" will pass according to the provisions of your will. Property held jointly with rights of survivorship, however, will pass automatically at your death to the surviving tenant, and will not be controlled by your will. Listing your assets helps you see how much you have. You will also see which assets can be transferred directly, which must be divided or converted to cash before they can be transferred, and which require special administration in order to reap any economic return.

As you take inventory, think of how you can make managing your estate less stressful for your heirs. If assets can be easily centralized into a few accounts instead of many, do it. If you own valuable personal property that is locked away somewhere, especially illiquid things such as art, jewelry, or antiques, consider disposing of all but the items you still hold dearest or that still give you pleasure. Then your heirs won't have to try to calculate what they are worth, or dispose of them under duress when they may get only a fraction of their value.

Beneficiary Designations

Unintended recipients and serious tax problems can leave your family devastated if you pass away before paying close attention to the beneficiary designations on your accounts (401K, pension, IRA, annuity accounts, deferred compensation, life insurance, etc.).

As an advisor, I have heard many cringe-worthy stories of situations where the paperwork wasn't updated, and thus accounts were distributed to a not-intended-for recipient.

Do NOT let that happen to you. Here's a list for review to see if your beneficiary documents need updating:

- Yes, I have a trust or my estate named as a beneficiary.

- Yes, I have been divorced.

- Yes, I have grandchildren by more than one of my children.

- Yes, I have a qualified retirement plan at work.

- Yes, I want a charity to get something from my estate upon death,

The Estate Planner's Toolkit

Here are some of the basic instruments used in estate planning:

Unlimited Marital Deduction

If you are married, the unlimited marital deduction allows spouses to transfer an unlimited amount of property at the first death without incurring a Federal gift or estate tax. This deduction can help alleviate the estate tax burden on the survivor; however, state inheritance and estate taxes may still apply. The deduction does not help you avoid the tax; it only delays it until the surviving spouse dies. When the surviving spouse dies, all the property that was previously shielded from taxation will be considered part of the taxable estate. Of course, any assets that were spent prior to the second death will not be taxed.

Annual Gift Program

A lifetime program of gift giving can increase the amount of property you can transfer without being taxed. In 2012, current law allows individuals to give up to $13,000 per year to a person without incurring any gift tax. This amount may increase in future years. In most cases, these gifts will not be included in the donor's estate, and will pass completely free of estate taxes as well. Another advantage of making annual gifts, particularly to young children, is that they result in income tax savings for the family. The future income from the gifted property will be taxed to the children at their income tax rates, which are usually lower than those of their parents or grandparents.

The other advantage of distributing assets prior to death is that the gifts may be more valuable to your children while you are alive than after you die. Children saving for a home, planning a big purchase, or simply facing financial difficulties, may find the smaller sums allowed as tax-free gifts more helpful than the larger sums you might leave them when you die.

Wills

The basic instrument of estate planning is the will; it is a legal document in which you state who will receive what portion of your property, as well as when and under what conditions they will receive it. A will also allows you to designate a guardian for your children, and an executor or personal representative who carries out the terms of the will. If you die intestate—without a will—the executor and guardian are appointed by the court, and your assets are disposed of according to state law. In all states, however, at least part of your estate will go to your children, and in many states, they will receive more than your spouse. A will that is complete and current, names all those with whom you would like to share in your estate, accounts for assets, and pays all creditors will ensure that the administration of your estate proceeds quickly and according to your intentions.

Keeping those close to you informed of your plans, especially if your financial or family situation changes, can help avoid litigation, costly delays, and unnecessary conflict.

Trusts

Trusts are vehicles that help you avoid probate, and depending on the type of trust used, might also shelter your assets from estate taxes. No trust, however, will protect you from having to pay income taxes, though the type of trust may also determine if you pay taxes at your own personal rate or at the higher trust rate. Trusts are a tool to manage the property that you leave to your heirs. Simply put, you transfer property in the name of a trustee who manages it for the benefit of a third party, the beneficiary. One of the great advantages of trusts is their flexibility. They can be adapted to fit a wide variety of situations. In fact, many attorneys say, "Trust is not the key word. Trust doesn't tell you that much." What *precedes* the word *trust* tells you everything. The most important aspect of trusts is that they allow property to be managed according to the donor's specific wishes, far into the future. Living trusts allow you to control trust assets; irrevocable trusts take away control but offer many attractive estate tax implications and more. No doubt, there is a type of trust that best suits your situation, and your advisor can help you determine which type of trust that might be.

Life Insurance

Life insurance is a flexible estate-planning tool that can be used to:

- Create an estate,

- Replace a financial loss caused by death,

- Provide liquidity to fund a business buyout agreement,

- Pay estate costs, or

- Transfer the cost of a charitable commitment.

Life insurance benefits are generally received income tax–free, and with careful planning can also be received estate-tax free. Since life insurance passes directly through to a beneficiary, it avoids the delays and expenses of probate. A survivorship or second (or last-to-die) insurance policy provides an ideal low-cost foundation for a married couple's estate plan. It is specifically designed to cover the costs of estate taxes and fees while insuring two lives under the same contract, and paying a benefit only upon the second or last death. Most sophisticated estate plans make optimal use of the unlimited marital deduction, and so defer the payment of estate taxes until the death of the surviving spouse.

A survivorship life insurance policy dovetails perfectly with these plans by providing the benefit when it is really needed. It provides a customized solution to the dilemma of estate taxes, and the need for liquidity.

Paying Costs

Even the most efficient estate planning will not totally eliminate state settlement costs. After using the tools that will minimize taxes and administration costs, you need to consider the alternatives for financing the remaining costs.

Four possible sources of funds can be used for these expenses: cash, credit, sale of assets, and life insurance.

1. **Cash.** Most estates don't normally have large cash reserves. Also, using cash resources costs the estate 100 cents on the dollar to pay the taxes.

2. **Credit.** The executor may obtain a bank loan at current interest rates. In certain cases, estates of closely held business interests might qualify for a loan from the Federal government for a portion of the estate settlement costs. With the interest total, estate settlement costs actually increase to more than 100 cents on the dollar.

3. **Sale of assets.** Having to sell non-liquid assets, such as securities, business interests, or real estate, can result in disastrous losses if markets are unfavorable. Additionally, commissions and other sales expenses could be incurred. Furthermore, if buyers know that you're desperate, you are unlikely to get fair market value for the assets you're trying to sell.

4. **Life insurance.** A life insurance policy provides cash immediately, and can be structured so that the proceeds pass to the beneficiary free of income, gift, and estate taxes. The result is that life insurance typically costs just pennies on the dollar to provide immediate funds to cover estate settlement costs by having the beneficiary use the proceeds to "buy" non-liquid assets from the estate, thus replacing non-liquid with liquid assets.

A tool for life insurance often used in estate planning is called the irrevocable life insurance trust or ILIT. Here, the trust, rather than an individual, owns the life insurance policy. ILITs offer many potential benefits, including:

- Death proceeds avoid Federal estate tax, generation-skipping taxes, or transfer taxes.

- Relatively small premium payments maximize the value of the annual gift tax exclusion since the entire policy proceeds will be sheltered from transfer tax.

- Estate liquidity problems can be solved.

- The estate left to heirs can be enhanced.

- Trust assets invested in life insurance avoid income tax.

- Death proceeds avoid the expenses and public aspect of probate.

- Death proceeds are managed for heirs by a trustee, according to the grantor's directions.

- Flexibility is still possible if the ILIT is properly designed.

One of the difficulties associated with life insurance trusts is that they may be irrevocable. However, some methods can increase flexibility. Today, ILITs can be structured in such a way that the proceeds are effectively removed from the estate, but are simultaneously accessible for living expenses. Clearly, the goal would be to *not* spend these assets. You would take distributions from the trust *only* as a last resort.

All of these strategies require the assistance of a qualified estate planning attorney that will be able to offer guidance on which approaches are best for your particular needs and situation. He/she designs the estate plan and oversees the plan's construction to assist the client in reaching the client's specific goals and objectives. The lawyer drafts all legal documents and provides all of the legal advice.

An estate plan can be as simple or complex as your situation warrants. But remember, there are only a few options for your money when you pass away.

Three things you can do with your money when you die

1. Give it to those you love.

2. Give it to organizations you care about.

3. Give it to the government.

Let's take them one by one.

Giving it to those you love

Many people who are considering an estate plan are in the midst of some truly golden years: They have grandchildren who may range from toddlers to young adults, and they cherish watching them grow. If there are young children in your extended family, and you want to make sure you support them in your estate plan, you should consider several attractive options.

Let's start with gifting, a particularly easy way to create a legacy for future generations by maximizing your annual gift exclusions. Right now, you can give $13,000 per year to any number of people without incurring gift taxes. You reduce the size of your estate, and shrink your exposure to estate taxes. And you can give those gifts to the same children and grandchildren who would be your heirs after your death. When you factor in the investment growth for those receiving the gifts, the impact of a consistent gift strategy can be significant.

Rate 6.00%

Annual Gift	# of Years Over Which Gifts Are Made				
	5	10	15	20	25
$13,000	$73,282.21	$171,350.33	$302,587.61	$478,212.69	$713,238.66
$26,000	$146,564.42	$342,700.67	$605,175.22	$956,425.37	$1,426,477.31
$39,000	$219,846.63	$514,051.00	$907,762.83	$1,434,638.06	$2,139,715.97
$52,000	$293,128.83	$685,401.34	$1,210,350.43	$1,912,850.74	$2,852,954.62
$65,000	$366,411.04	$856,751.67	$1,512,938.04	$2,391,063.43	$3,566,193.28
$78,000	$439,693.25	$1,028,102.01	$1,815,525.65	$2,869,276.11	$4,279,431.94
$91,000	$512,975.46	$1,199,452.34	$2,118,113.26	$3,347,488.80	$4,992,670.59
$104,000	$586,257.67	$1,370,802.67	$2,420,700.87	$3,825,701.49	$5,705,909.25
$117,000	$659,539.88	$1,542,153.01	$2,723,288.48	$4,303,914.17	$6,419,147.90
$130,000	$732,822.08	$1,713,503.34	$3,025,876.09	$4,782,126.86	$7,132,386.56

Assumption of 6 percent return over 25 years.

Consider a generation-skipping trust. If your children are financially secure, you may choose a trust arrangement that skips a generation entirely, leaving substantial assets to your grandchildren. You avoid two generations of estate taxes, and leave greater assets intact for your grandchildren. These funds will grow with investment returns over ten, fifteen or twenty years while your grandchildren also grow and mature.

An insurance trust is another valuable option in estate planning. By transferring small amounts of your estate (usually equal to an insurance premium) into an irrevocable life insurance trust, you can reduce your current estate while creating a much larger asset outside the estate. The transfers can be funded by your annual $13,000 gift tax exemption, and the proceeds of the policy would not be subject to estate taxes or income taxes, so those you designate would receive the full amount of the policy.

Here's an example of how you can use life insurance. A client in her early sixties recently inherited $500,000. She and her husband were thrilled, but the money soon became a source of stress. She dearly loved their two sons, and was determined to pass the full $500,000 on to them when she died, so the couple invested the money conservatively, spent very little, and lived frugally. While her commitment to the next generation was strong, she and her husband were frustrated that they could not enjoy their retirement more. They sought guidance, and as a result, the couple purchased a $500,000 life insurance policy, naming the sons as the beneficiaries. The couple paid the insurance premiums from the investment returns on the inheritance, and soon they were living a much happier retirement. They traveled, played golf more, and enjoyed the reassurance that they had taken the right steps to pass on a meaningful legacy.

Give it to organizations you care about

For many people, a strong motivation for financial planning is the desire to share our wealth or good fortune with others beyond the tight circle of those we love most dearly. That compelling sense of responsibility for others, even those we may not know, appears to be an innate drive in many human beings. It is one of the principal tenets of every major religion and nearly every society, whether primitive or modern. It is an acknowledgment of the spiritual nature of people, providing a common bond that we are all God's children—and the intensely social nature of human beings where no man is an island.

Every year we see examples of the desire to help others. In 2005, it was the devastating tsunami in the Indian Ocean. The flow of contributions to relief efforts was staggering. The empathy we so obviously felt for those few who survived in many coastal villages even compelled Congress to take the extraordinary step of allowing contributions to tsunami relief made up until January 31, 2005, to be deductible on 2004 tax returns. In 2010 it was the terrible earthquake in Haiti, which killed hundreds of thousands of people, and to which Americans gave almost half a billion dollars. Again, Congress allowed charitable contributions to Haitian relief to be tax deductible in 2010 even if they were made after year end. And while charitable contributions dropped during the 2008 recession, they're climbing steadily back to pre-crisis levels; as jobs and incomes return, so are donations to the even less fortunate.

Charities, Faith Communities, Colleges, and Causes: Little Planning Required

Our propensity to share our wealth with others finds its expression most often in support of charities, faith communities, colleges, and causes. Most people's motivation is purely altruistic. Many of my clients make very generous contributions to each of these types of organizations simply because they believed it was right to share their wealth. In most cases, they didn't know those they were helping, and certainly expected nothing in return. If any self-interest was involved, it was simply that they wanted a better world for themselves and their children.

For many, most charitable giving is a matter of routine. They plan each week, month, or year to contribute a certain amount of money to an organization or cause that is important to them. Even if they are "tithers" who regularly give 10 percent of their income to church or charity, that giving is a matter of course for them. Many view it as nondiscretionary spending. It is as much a part of their financial obligations as paying their utility bills every month. They treat giving much as I recommend you treat investing: They set aside a percentage of their income every month before they address other spending or saving possibilities.

In that respect, giving is for most people not necessarily a part of their financial planning process. It becomes a more important issue in planning, however, for those with greater personal net worth who want to make larger gifts or bequests to the organizations they favor. They can establish trusts or foundations that make their contributions more efficient for them, as well as for the benefiting institutions.

Unless you have significant assets of over six figures to establish a trust, that form of giving will probably be inefficient for you to continue to make your regular, usually tax-deductible, gifts as you see fit. This section on giving is shorter, based on the very nature of most giving, and not because it is less important to share your wealth than to spend it on yourself.

If you are facing a major financial event, such as the sale of valuable property or inheriting money, investigate all available tools to see how to include organizations you like.

The other prime opportunity to investigate a giving strategy is when you prepare your will. If you wish to leave some portion of your estate to a charitable organization, consult your financial advisor or the organization directly to find out how to make that gift most efficiently for you both. Most charities, faith communities, colleges, and causes have their own experts in gift giving, and can provide sound advice.

Giving Your Time and Energy

Another form of sharing your wealth may benefit significantly from careful financial planning. Especially in retirement, many people want to be able to do volunteer work, sharing their energy or expertise. This presumes that you have planned well enough to retire at an age when you are still sufficiently healthy and financially secure to devote time and energy to a favored cause.

In the following section I will address briefly some of the ways that you and your causes may benefit from the establishment of charitable trusts.

Charitable Trusts

Charitable trusts were provided for in the U.S. tax code for one simple reason: to encourage you to contribute to organizations that address our nation's or our world's needs, so that governments do not have to be involved. Our nation's leaders have always recognized the importance of private citizens and nonprofit organizations addressing the pressing needs of our society and our world. That is why charitable giving is tax deductible, and that is why rules for giving through trusts were created by our Federal and state governments.

Like everything else in our tax code, the rules for charitable trusts are complicated. But it is worth playing by IRS rules because you may gain significant tax advantages by giving through a trust. Does that lessen the altruism of your gift? Not at all. In fact, the tax benefits inherent in giving the IRS way likely enable you to give more than you would otherwise feel comfortable doing.

A gift made to an eligible organization is deductible on your income taxes however it is made, as an outright cash gift or as part of a charitable trust, within some percentage limits. Gifts made to charitable organizations in almost every form may also reduce the size of your estate, whether given during your lifetime or through your estate, and may therefore reduce any estate tax your heirs might have to pay. Gifts made through trusts may also offer the advantage of avoiding capital gains taxes on highly appreciated assets.

One of the primary advantages of charitable trusts is that they may allow you to make charitable gifts during your lifetime, instead of waiting to make a contribution through your estate. This is a dilemma for many people because they might depend on income from their assets to meet their daily needs. Or with an unpredictable future, they can't be sure what resources they will consume in their lifetime. They could keep their assets, and simply specify in their will that they want so much money to go to such and such organization.

The advantage of a charitable trust created during your lifetime is that your gift goes to work sooner for the beneficiary of your trust—and you have the opportunity to see your gift at work and the tax benefits accrue to you, rather than just your estate.

That is why split-interest gifts are allowed through trusts. Split-interest gifts refer to assets that have two valuable parts: One is an asset, the other is the income that asset is able to earn. In a split-interest gift, one portion is given in trust for the charity, and the other portion is retained. In other words, you may give an asset to a charity through a trust, but retain the income which that asset earns until your death. This is called a *remainder trust*. When you die, or after a set period of time, the asset and the income become the property of the charity. The other possibility is to give the income from the asset to charity—*a lead trust*—but retain ownership of the underlying asset that earns the income.

- Example: Let's say you bought 10,000 shares of some cheap stock in 1965. That stock has split many times, and pays a handsome dividend, which now provides much of your retirement income. It has appreciated in value many times over. If you established a remainder trust using those shares of stock, you would enjoy many benefits. You would:

  - Still receive the dividend income from that stock for your lifetime, available to pay your living expenses.

  - Not have to pay capital gains tax on the huge appreciation of that stock since you bought it.

  - Be able to claim a charitable deduction on your taxes for the present value of the charitable remainder of donated stock in the year you contribute to the trust. In addition, you avoid tax on the capital gain, and you still receive income from that asset. The likely result is a reduction in the income tax you owe.

- Have reduced the size of your estate, so your heirs will owe less estate tax, if any.

- Have given a valuable asset to your favorite charity that it will own when you die—asset, income, and all.

Those are significant benefits for you and the charity, and well worth getting the professional assistance required to establish a trust.

How Much Do You Need?

Unless you have in the neighborhood of $250,000 to put into a trust, it probably would not be efficient.

A trust is a separate legal entity that must file its own tax returns and requires other paperwork, which will probably cost at least $2,000 a year. With much less than $250,000 in the trust, these costs probably take too high a percentage of the trust's value to justify them.

An alternative to establishing your own trust is to contribute to a *pooled income fund* (PIF). PIFs operate like a trust, but combine the gifts of many people. If you would like to make a contribution to a charity through a trust, but have insufficient funds to justify the administrative costs on your own, check if your favorite charity already created a PIF to which you could contribute. Many charities have PIFs, would welcome your contribution, and will make it very easy for you to contribute.

Donor-Advised Funds

Another alternative vehicle for charitable giving is a Donor-Advised Fund (DAF). A donor-advised fund is a separately identified fund or account that is maintained by a sponsoring organization, which could be organizations such as for-profit financial services companies, community foundations, and other not-for-profit organizations. Donor-advised funds offer many of the same benefits of charitable trusts, but are less expensive due to the sponsoring organization's ability to aggregate donors to keep costs down. A person who is charitably inclined can make a tax-deductible contribution to the fund, be it in cash, appreciated securities, or other assets. He or she can then direct how the fund is to be invested to grow the account until a charitable contribution is directed to be made from the fund. The donor may then make donations to qualified 501(c)(3) organizations over time from the fund. Donor-advised funds are popular because they provide a better alternative for smaller donations, as well as providing tax incentives.

Planning With the Charity of Your Choice

Whether you choose to create a trust yourself or a donor-advised fund, or take part in a *pooled income fund*, charitable organizations know the rules, and can explain the benefits and procedures. Why do charities like to be the beneficiaries of charitable trusts, and often prefer them to cash gifts? It's quite simple from their perspective as well:

- A trust establishes a dependable income stream on which the charity can base future plans.

- A trust provides some predictability regarding the amount of money the organization will receive on a regular basis.

So the charitable organization will be as helpful as possible in removing any obstacles between you and your potential gift.

One word of caution on establishing charitable trusts with the assistance of the charity itself. Unlike a personal financial advisor, the financial pros at your charity may not fully understand your overall financial goals and plans apart from your desire to make a charitable contribution.

*Even with the best of intentions,
the charity's advisors may not have a good enough
grasp of your financial big picture to help you make your
gift as efficient as possible for you, and for them,
thus it's important to work with your own
financial professionals.*

Give it to the government

Of the three things you can do with your money when you die, paying estate tax is the one you want to do least, if at all. However, I did meet a man who had served our country, and he was happy to let the government have his money upon his death because he felt the government had done a lot for him. In any event, I think it's important that you know what estate tax is, and if you've had good estate planning, you won't be paying more than your fair share.

The estate tax is a tax imposed on the transfer of property from a deceased person to heirs or other recipients of the estate. The property can be transferred through a will or testament, which is a legally enforceable document directing the disposal of a decedent's property. If there is no will (and if you've done estate planning, this won't be the case), property is transferred according to the state laws of intestacy, which means dying without a will—or as a consequence of the death of the owner, as in payment of life insurance benefits or money from 401(k) or IRA accounts.

The starting point for what is taxable is called the "gross estate." The gross estate is property transferred, or considered transferred, at death, including bank accounts, stocks, bonds, mutual funds, IRAs, retirement accounts, real estate, collectibles, and the death benefit of any life insurance policies that were owned by the decedent. Even items that are usually exempt from income taxes, like life insurance benefits, are included in the gross estate, and increase its amount.

After you have determined the gross estate, you can then claim deductions for funeral expenses, administration expenses, debts, charitable contributions, estate taxes paid to states, and certain property that is left to the surviving spouse. The remainder is then compared to the current Federal Estate Tax exemption amount of $5,120,000, with excess taxed at rates as high as 35 percent. (The exemption amount is set by Congress, and has been in flux over the past five years. It can, and probably will, change.) Some states, like Minnesota and New York, have lower exemption amounts. And some states don't just tax the excess of the estate above the exemption amount, they tax the entire estate from the first dollar once your estate goes above a certain threshold.

The personal representative or executor of the estate must file an IRS form 706 for estate taxes, along with payment of any applicable taxes, within nine months of the date of death if the estate is above the Federal Estate Tax exemption. IRS form 706 is filed separately from your personal income tax return.

That's the basics of how estate taxes work. If you're actually involved in settling an estate, you'll of course want to go beyond this information and talk to an attorney who specializes in trusts and estates.

If you're just beginning your estate planning, take this section like a warning sign on the journey: Do the right thing, and nothing bad will happen.

CHAPTER 5

The Five Things You Can Do With Your Money, and How to Do Them Right

Let's start this very important discussion with an example of what not to do.

As a financial advisor, I take great pride in hoping for the best—and planning for the worst. I tell my clients that they must prepare for the certainty of uncertainty, and the reality is that no one, including me, knows what will happen tomorrow, next week, next month, or next year. And there's no better example than the Great Recession that began in 2008, when no investments performed well.

It was virtually impossible to make money in 2008 because all asset classes were down at the same time. But 2008 was a very rare year, the likes of which we don't expect to see often in our lifetime. Now as I write this, about every fifteen minutes on most radio stations, you will hear a commercial of some company trying to sell gold. Because of the volatile stock market of the last decade, many people have lost confidence in the stock market, and they think they need to find alternative investments to stocks. For a lot of people, gold is the solution. Many companies have jumped on the bandwagon, taking advantage of naïve consumers or investors who are trying to make a profit by selling them what they think they want.

Many believe gold offers protection against rising interest rates, and that gold will go up if the stock market goes down. But there's no proof of that. Gold, silver, and other precious metals are speculative investments, and returns are not guaranteed. Consider the rush on gold in the late 1970s and early 1980s when, at that point, we had runaway inflation. On the New York Mercantile Exchange, gold prices reached a then-record high of $850 an ounce, and by the time prices peaked in January of 1980, the commodity seemed like a can't-miss investment. However, for 235 straight months—nearly twenty years— gold prices dropped. It finally bottomed out at $253 an ounce in July of 1999. It took another 7½ years, until around 2007, for the prices to return to the January 1980 high.

Can you imagine any stock investment or any bond investment where you had to wait twenty-seven years to get it back to even? And gold does not pay dividends or interest. And although stocks can pay dividends as do bonds, stocks can split so one share can become two. Gold cannot do any of these things.

We have no evidence that gold can protect against rising interest rates or low stock prices or inflation. If true, gold prices and interest rates would be what we call "positively correlated," meaning when interest rates rise, then gold prices should also rise. But the two are not consistently correlated, and gold and interest rates, or gold and inflation, or gold and stocks, have no proven correlation. Gold seems to have a mind of its own.

Also, gold will not necessarily protect you from a weak dollar, which occurs when the value of the U.S. dollar declines in value when compared to other foreign currency, such as the Euro, the British Pound, or the Japanese Yen. When this happens, some people stock up on gold because they believe gold and the dollar have "negative correlation," meaning when one rises the other falls. But that also has not proven to be true.

Over the past nearly fifty years, gold has moved in the opposite direction of the dollar only about 20 percent of the time. At our firm, precious metals are not considered one of our four core asset classes, which we identify as stocks, bonds, real estate, and cash. However, this doesn't mean you should never own gold, silver, or other precious metals, as they can be a tactical overlay as part of a broadly diversified portfolio.

The problem is that many investors look at gold, and stocks, too, for that matter, as all or nothing. Frequently people call our radio show saying, "I'm out of the market right now. Do you think it's time to get back in?" or "I'm in the market right now. Do you think it's going to go down, and I should get out?" The reality is that I never recommend "all or nothing."

When I recommend alterations to portfolios, I might change an asset class from 20 percent to 10 percent or 30 percent, but it will never go to zero, and it will never go to 100 percent. Having a small percentage of gold in the mix may be appropriate, but it would be insanity for an investor to sell all of his or her stocks, or all other investments, and put it all into gold.

In recent years, gold has outpaced most other asset classes. If an investor had been smart enough to buy gold a few years ago, he or she would have done well indeed. But looking at long-term history, gold and other precious metals have actually not performed as well as stocks, and have been more volatile. Never in a twenty-seven-year period of time would you have failed to make money on your investment in stocks, such as what occurred in gold from 1980 to 2006.

Options for your wealth

Your options for what to do with your money may seem as boundless as the prairie sky I grew up under, but in truth they are limited because you can really do only five things with money:

1. Spend it.

2. Save it.

3. Invest it.

4. Pay taxes with it.

5. Give it away.

Slice the pie however you'd like, but those five pieces are your options, and for most people, only spending and paying taxes are mandatory. Our basic needs require spending, which means no one is completely self-sufficient in that they produce, make, or barter for everything they need to live. Everyone spends something.

Despite the talk of extremely wealthy or extremely poor people who pay no taxes, it is almost impossible not to pay some tax. Your income will almost certainly be taxed. But taxes are not as ironclad as many think, and it is neither illegal nor unethical to reduce your tax with opportunities provided by the U.S. tax code.

The other three categories—saving, investing, and giving—are completely voluntary. Many people have chosen, to their detriment, not to cut their pie into that many pieces, no matter how big or small the pie.

Few of us have the resources to do everything we would like with our money, so we need to establish priorities. We have to clearly understand our options, and how they interact. A bigger slice for spending reduces the size of all the other slices, except paying taxes. On the other hand, *less* spending may increase the size of the investing or giving/donating slices, which may also decrease the size of the tax slice.

The objective of financial planning is to increase our control of the size of each slice.

Spending: What Do You Want, and When Do You Want It?

For most people, spending takes up the major part of their income. Almost no one has so much money that they don't have to be concerned about spending. What about the super rich? Curious, isn't it, that some of the greatest corporate scandals of recent times have been perpetrated by people who were already wealthy beyond the imaginations of most of us. Why? Only they and their shrinks could make a good guess. I suspect it's partly because they wanted to spend more. Strange as it seems, there is always more to buy.

You have probably played this game. You ponder how much money you'd have to have before you quit working (or want more). Most of us set realistic guidelines, but some people cannot be satisfied with what they have, and want more.

Necessities or Luxuries

Most every dollar you spend falls into two simple categories: necessities and luxuries. The challenge of dividing our spending in such a way, however, is made more difficult because of the simple fact that most of us are not now, and never have been, in dire need.

Still, a "necessities versus luxuries" spending breakdown is useful for anyone trying to organize his or her finances, and use money efficiently. Most people spend the largest share of their money, as opposed to saving, investing, or giving it away. Therefore, whether you are buying necessities or luxuries, spending has to be the starting point for any financial planning. A dollar not spent is a dollar that can be used in another way; a dollar not spent has the same future value as an extra dollar earned.

You can increase the size of your financial pie only three ways:

1. Spending less,

2. Earning more, or

3. In some cases, paying less tax.

There is no baseline for needs or wants. One person's needs are another's luxuries. You just have to look at analyses of the "basics" of living in the United States to see the evolution in what we consider necessities. Necessities gradually include the modern conveniences that technology has made available.

- When did a smart phone, and certainly cell phones, become a necessity instead of a luxury in our scrambled lives? I would bet that many people who have become accustomed to their phones at their sides, in their pockets, or in their purses would have a very difficult time living without them—at least for awhile.

- Is a car a necessity or a luxury? Depends on where you live, what you do for a living, and what access you have to public transportation. In most parts of the country, cars are a necessity. You couldn't live in Southern California very easily without a car. The same is true in my home area, the Twin Cities of St. Paul and Minneapolis, Minnesota, although some people here still rely primarily on buses, bicycles, and walking. Many residents of New York or Boston, on the other hand, live quite comfortably without a car. How nice a car do you need to get to work or to carry the kids to piano lessons? Many people could spend $10,000 or $20,000 less on their vehicles, and still meet their basic transportation needs.

- What about food and drink? We have to eat and drink to live, but what exactly are we choosing to eat and drink? A stop for an expensive cup of coffee on the way to work is how many start their day. A necessity? Is habit synonymous with need?

- Is wine a necessity? For some people, a glass of wine with dinner is not viewed as a luxury, but part of their cultural tradition.

- What about the vast array of specialty home appliances? How necessary are they? Certainly we can prepare food for ourselves and our families without microwave ovens. But what if the time we save cooking is spent with our kids, enriching their lives, or enriching our lives in other ways?

- What is the line in the sand between necessity and luxury? What about a home computer? Television? If TV is a necessity, does that include cable TV service like ESPN or CNN?

- And what about pets? Now we have many options for pet food, toys, and health products. Some people would claim that their pets are important members of their families, providing companionship for the elderly, and lessons in responsibility for children.

These points are raised not to chide people for how they spend money, but rather to help us understand our own spending patterns and habits.

We need to understand without reservation that we have many more choices than we think when it comes to using our money.

Everyone will arrive at different conclusions as to what is a necessity and what is a luxury. The psychology of "need" is a complex subject, and indeed, some people may have unusual needs. We hear about such examples in the media every day.

Some people blame advertising for manufacturing "needs" in our society. Observe a child watching public television shows without any advertising, and compare it to when he is exposed to commercial programs. Seeing the ads, the child realizes there are many things he or she really must have.

Our susceptibility to advertising, and the needs it creates, doesn't make advertising itself the culprit. What if someone invents, develops, or improves a product? Wouldn't you want to know? We all have the ability to resist the needs that advertising supposedly creates. We always have choices. How we make them is solely our responsibility.

This scenario distinguishing needs from wants is irrelevant for most of us because our affluence and our lifestyles are so far removed from "actual survival." The question becomes not what we need to live, but what we need to be happy. Regardless of your attitudes about spending on luxuries now, your "needs" will inevitably grow with time, affluence, and invention.

Some people have chosen to opt out of our material world and live simpler lives. More power to them if they are happier that way, but even those people become dependent to a degree on the needs and wants of others.

A friend who spent several years working in Africa framed the challenge as follows. In many African societies there is a vigorous debate about the extent to which they should adopt "Western" customs or maintain their traditional cultures. The critical question becomes, "Do you want your children to live?" Do you then need hospitals, roads, schools, buses, basic hygiene, clean water, and sewage treatment? If you want your children to live better, then you need much of what modern technology offers. This means you move beyond an agrarian, barter economy to one that requires capital formation, skilled labor, and, in many cases, a significant step away from traditional means of governance.

How we answer these questions tells a great deal about our view of money, as well as our use of it to get what we want both now and in the future.

Now or Later?

The second spending issue is not what we need, but when? Do we spend to keep ourselves alive and healthy today, and save any remaining resources for future needs? Or do we spend our money on luxuries and resources that are above those needed to survive today?

An ancient fable tells the story of an ant and a grasshopper. The industrious ant saved for the winter, storing mounds of grain. The grasshopper did not, playing his fiddle all day instead of working to put away the harvest. When winter snows came, the ant had food, but the grasshopper did not. Finally, the ant took in the grasshopper and fed him. The story had a happy ending when the grasshopper's fiddling provided entertainment for all the ants. He ultimately had a skill that earned him his keep.

The fable is intended to emphasize the necessity to plan ahead, but some could also view the story as redemption for the grasshopper: He developed a skill that luckily he could barter for food.

Choosing how and when we spend our money is not much different from the ant and the grasshopper choosing how to spend their time. We can live for today or live for the rest of our lives. I am not suggesting that you live like a pauper today so that you won't have to in retirement. Neither option is very attractive. But if you have an understanding of your spending, you can begin to strike a balance that's right for you. You can learn to use money more effectively, given your habits, your foibles, and your strengths.

For many people, financial success will require delaying some gratification, which doesn't come naturally to a lot of people. Maybe it is an innate personality trait, some gene that determines our propensity to spend today or save for tomorrow. The evidence is in small children. Some readily put aside some candy for another day, whereas other kids think that notion would be preposterous. Did the kids who delay gratification learn it from their parents' urgings? I'm not so certain. I wouldn't be surprised to read someday that a geneticist has discovered a pinchpenny gene in humans.

The Propensity to Consume

Most people and most societies consume what they can. Americans are notoriously shortsighted, as demonstrated by a personal savings rate that is low by international standards. There could be many explanations, from a standard of affluence that has distanced us from the struggle for mere survival, to our propensity to invent and create that places a premium on spending whatever money we have in order to create and consume more. We are a consumer society. Just look at the ads. What percent sell luxuries?

Here's an example from the financial planning business. A client couple had a combined income of $70,000 a year, and had managed to annually save 10 percent for retirement. Now both had received raises, increasing their income by $7,000. Should they add all of that increase to their savings, save 10 percent of the additional amount, or spend it and continue saving $7,000 a year as they did before, effectively reducing their savings rate to 9 percent? After our discussions, they decided to spend all the additional income on purchases they had put off when they were making less. They continued to save, just at a lower level, even though they had more disposable income.

- **Exercise:** Track your spending. Try to remember every expenditure, no matter how small. Keep track of what you spend, recording it daily in a little notebook for a week or a month. You may be surprised to find that you are guilty of having a habit, one that means you never have money. Some people who constantly feel money pressure will buy little treats or rewards, in part because they never have the money to buy what they really want. But it's precisely that accumulation of "little" expenses that prevents them from getting ahead. Many don't even realize they do this. As you track your expenditures, add them up in different categories at the end of your test period: food and drink, entertainment, utilities, gifts, and so forth. Pay particular attention to the small expenditures on unnecessary items, and you'll see how they accumulate over time.

Consumer Debt: The Silent Thief of Wealth

Spending too much is one thing if you have the money to spend. Spending it when you do not have it—going into debt—is quite another. Debt can be the thief of dreams. Used wisely, debt can make your life richer. Used poorly, it may lead you to a life of money worries.

Consumer debt is like driving on a highway through Death Valley where you see signs that say the next services are fifty-some miles away. Once you're on that highway, you don't have many chances to get off or get help.

I repeat this admonition, as do all other financial advisors, only because it is so critical to your financial success. If you can't pay off your credit card bills when they arrive each month, you shouldn't use credit cards. They are wonderful as a convenience, but that convenience has led many people down a very dangerous road.

Don't even go into a store unless you have the cash in hand. And in these uncertain economic times, don't even assume that you will have enough to pay for an item as soon as you get your next paycheck. Your next paycheck might be your last, if you are laid off. Cash in hand means dollars, hard currency, in your pocket, not the likelihood or expectation that you will have it.

Imagine the opportunity cost of consumer debt. You're not only paying interest, but also forfeiting the ability to earn a return on those dollars if you could have invested them. The cost of consumer debt becomes staggering—and the only purpose it serves for most people is to enable them to buy things a few months earlier than if they had saved the money to pay in cash.

If you have consumer debt, with interest rates these days in the 10 percent to 20 percent range, you are essentially paying 10 percent to 20 percent more for every purchase you make until you pay off that debt. Any dollar you spend, instead of applying it toward your balance, is a borrowed dollar. If you're using a credit card to buy a $1.50 loaf of bread, it's actually costing you $1.80 if you have a credit balance at 20 percent interest. The interest paid on those purchases will, in the long run, even buying things on 15 percent discount, make them no bargain if you pay 20 percent interest.

Consumer debt is the first thing any financial plan should address. For millions of Americans, consumer debt and personal bankruptcies are at all-time highs. People carry balances on high-interest credit cards, and never seem to gain ground. They cannot eliminate that debt—and they have a devil of a time even reducing it.

I have seen firsthand how deep a hole some people can dig for themselves with consumer debt. One of the more extreme examples was a couple I'll call Phil and Lil who came to me because they wanted to purchase their dream home. The home cost $350,000, which wasn't out of their reach because they had a combined annual income of $150,000. But when they went to get financing for the house, several lenders turned them down. The reason? Combined, they had more than $100,000 of credit card debt—money for which they were paying, on average, 16 percent interest. Result: Every month the interest cost alone on that debt, without paying a penny toward the principal, was more than $1,300.

Most Americans do not have that much of a problem with credit cards/plastic money, but some people have debt at levels that will keep them from *ever* investing a penny, unless they radically change their spending habits.

The first step in controlling debt is to control spending.
Stop debt from growing.

Step 1: Cut off debts' fuel. Keeping up with the Joneses is dangerous, and can cause irreparable financial harm. Just because your neighbor bought a new jungle gym for his children, you don't have to. Remember that credit cards are not a replacement for cash. Waiting a few months for that new bedroom furniture or going without a vacation this year will not be easy, but postponing those purchases will better serve you in the long run.

Step 2: Pay it off. People know they should be saving, and then investing for retirement or buying a home, causing them to save a small sum from their paychecks. But those same people are paying relatively high interest on credit card balances. Every dollar those people save—instead of using it to pay off their credit cards—loses money for them. Why? Because very few investments will consistently pay a return higher than many credit card rates. If you earn, as an example, 12 percent on your investments, which is a good return compared to the historical average for the stock market, but you are paying 18 percent interest on a credit card, you are actually losing 6 percent a year on your investment—before taxes. Why would you invest in anything where you are so likely to see your money dwindle? That is inefficient, to say the least.

Step 3: Pay off your consumer debt even if doing so means that you *save nothing*. It is one of the best ways to use your money. Once those monthly credit card payments are gone, you will be amazed at how fast you can save money.

Many people cannot afford to pay cash for a car these days. This is the one case when most people will take on some debt to purchase something that will not appreciate in value. But to my knowledge, it is the only consumer purchase that justifies taking on debt. What about a home? See the next section.

Good Debt: Mortgages

Is debt always bad? No. There is such a thing as "good" debt, and it has four characteristics:

1. Good debt is receiving a lower interest rate than you may earn on your investments.

2. Good debt is useful for buying assets that will likely increase in value, and you enjoy the full appreciation of that asset. Or for self-improvement that may increase your personal income potential and marketability.

3. Good debt means that interest payments may be tax deductible.

4. Good debt allows amortization if done over a long period of time.

Only a home mortgage meets all these criteria. Student loans also come close to meeting these criteria in that you pay a low interest rate, and they help you buy an asset that should increase your earning power for the rest of your life. Another possible exception is an investment in your business or profession, but that really fits into the category of business finance, not personal finance.

The government makes a home mortgage one of the most efficient obligations. The mortgage-interest deduction is the biggest tax deduction for most people—and by far the biggest of all government subsidies. Your home mortgage interest tax deduction makes it an extremely effective way to borrow and *invest* money.

Generally, buying a home represents a good debt, and is also probably the best investment many people will ever make. The housing run-up from 2003 to 2006 was over-exuberant, and we saw a correction in lower real estate values.

We saw nearly unprecedented decreases in home values from 2007 to 2010. That said, we had unprecedented increases in home values from 1995 to 2007. Homes should and will appreciate in value over a long period of time, but it is illogical to assume that rate of appreciation would be anything much greater than the pace of inflation. We would anticipate home values on the average to increase somewhere between 3 to 6 percent per year, depending upon location, neighborhoods, school districts, and so forth.

What we saw from 2007 to 2010, I believe, was probably a-once-in-a-lifetime aberration, but so was what we saw in terms of increases and run-up in home prices in the early 2000s. When we do future value forecasting, we typically assume about a 4 percent appreciation rate for the long-term expectation for an increase in the home's value. One caution about the inevitability of rising home prices in the long run: It depends on inflation and a few other factors that contribute to inflation, like rising real wages, growing population, and a finite amount of land. Should there be deflation, the last thing you want is a fixed-rate mortgage because your payment remains the same while your wages decline. Deflation is unlikely in the U.S., but not impossible as is witnessed by Japan's more than a decade of inflation between the early 1990s and 2006.

Making "Good" into "Better"

Even if the house you buy does not appreciate in value, you are still able to enjoy the single greatest tax break available by deducting mortgage interest from your taxes while you live in your house.

Of course, even if you want to take advantage of the economic and "quality-of-life" advantages of home ownership, you still have many important decisions to make about the type of financing.

What type of mortgage is best? *The longest term at the lowest rate, with the lowest down payment without paying points.* A mortgage is the cheapest money you can borrow. Long-term, investments in equities historically have earned higher rates of return than current mortgage interest rates. If you have the discipline to invest the difference between a longer-term monthly payment and the payment on a shorter-term mortgage, the longer mortgage should leave you in a better position for long-term investing.

Buying the use of money today through a mortgage is so efficient that I recommend making the smallest possible down payment when you buy a house, and carrying the largest mortgage that you can. Consider this: Today you could get a thirty-year fixed mortgage for about 3 percent to 4 percent interest. Depending on your tax bracket, after taking your interest deduction, your net "cost" of that money would have been 2 to 3 percent. Could you have invested the extra money not used for a down payment, and then averaged better than 3 percent net after taxes? Probably, and many people have.

A simpler way to think about this is to disregard taxes. In other words, you finance at 4 percent, and don't consider the deduction. The historical average annual return of the S&P 500 from 1999 to 2011 is nearly 8 percent. Economically it makes sense to try to invest as soon as possible, and apply less money to your mortgage debt. Using these hypothetical figures, you would have a net pretax gain on these dollars of almost 4 percent.

The price of borrowing money fluctuates, of course, as does the price of anything else. If mortgage interest rates were to rise again above 10 percent, as they did in the 1980s, you would have to carefully compare the potential net gain or loss of any down payment or prepayment plan. But if you financed or refinanced in recent years at around 4 percent interest, you may do better by investing that money instead of paying down your mortgage

But, you say, what if you figure in the appreciation of the real estate? That has to be worth something. It is—but your home will appreciate at the same rate, regardless of how much equity you have in it. It does not appreciate faster if you have more equity. In fact, if your home does appreciate, you earn a far higher return on your investment if your down payment is *lower*.

Suppose you are going to purchase a home for $200,000. You can actually get financing with 5 percent down, or $10,000, but you're considering putting down $40,000, or 20 percent. What will happen if your home appreciates by 5 percent the first year? You would have $10,000 of appreciation. Therefore, with $10,000 down, you would have a return on equity of 100 percent. With a down payment of $40,000, however, your return on equity would be only 25 percent.

One catch in making lower down payments is that many lenders require mortgage insurance until the borrower has 20 percent equity in the property. Look carefully at the cost of that mortgage insurance to compare it with the cost of a lower down payment. Or better yet, find a mortgage lender that does not require mortgage insurance. Some home buyers have even found that it's cheaper to immediately take out a second mortgage to cover the difference between the down payment and the 20 percent equity requirement, just to eliminate the high premiums of mortgage insurance.

Take a good look, especially if you are paying mortgage insurance because you have less than 20 percent equity in your home. Has your home appreciated in value enough that you would have 20 percent equity at your home's current market price? If so, call your mortgage holder to learn how to get rid of the mortgage insurance. They will likely require only a new appraisal of your home to establish its current value. In most parts of the country a full appraisal costs around $400. If you are paying $50 a month in mortgage insurance, you will pay for the cost of that appraisal in eight months if you can eliminate your mortgage insurance. After that, you have an extra $50 a month to spend, save, or invest.

A 15-Year vs. a 30-Year Mortgage

The logic we applied to you making the smallest down payment possible, without incurring additional costs, also applies to the term of your mortgage. Should you take a fifteen-year or a thirty-year mortgage? With the low interest rates of recent years, many people have been able to afford the larger monthly payments of a shorter-duration mortgage. Therefore, they have opted for a fifteen-year mortgage to eliminate the debt twice as fast, and save thousands in interest costs. That's a bad choice—at least if you have the discipline to take the difference in the monthly payments—and invest it.

Even though a loan may be amortized over a thirty-year period, nothing prevents us from paying it off early. If we take a thirty-year mortgage and invest the difference between the smaller payment and what our payment would have been on a fifteen-year mortgage schedule, we actually need only a very modest rate of return in order to make a balloon payment to pay off our thirty-year mortgage in fifteen years or less.

Prepaying Your Mortgage

After going through this complicated explanation of how you could perhaps pay off your mortgage early, and come out ahead by investing money for fifteen years, instead of increasing your monthly payments, I want you to disregard it. Why? Because I don't think prepaying a mortgage makes good financial sense. For those with the discipline to invest the money they could use to prepay their mortgage, I recommend *against* prepaying the mortgage. We have already seen that you may come out ahead investing instead of taking a shorter-duration mortgage. We have seen that after fifteen years of investment returns below even close-to-historical averages for the S&P 500, you would be ahead by investing. Now double the period to thirty years. The argument for not prepaying your mortgage becomes even stronger.

Of course, all of these benefits disappear if you don't have the discipline to invest "the difference." In addition, you need to consider the risk involved in investing; the returns will fluctuate, with the possibility of loss of principal. If by seeing others suffer a foreclosure, it forces you to set aside money monthly, you're better off to take the shorter mortgage. If you don't have the discipline now to invest, you may never get far enough ahead to even think about saving and investing.

But if you're my client, it is my *job* to help you become a better manager of your money, and not acquiesce to inefficient behavior—or simply do whatever seems easiest. Yes, we are consumers, and the human inclination is to spend. But that does not mean consuming is good for you. I'm describing smart money management, not easy money management, and if needed, will encourage you to change your money habits. I can't smugly tell you to do what is not in your best interest just because I have doubts about whether you can follow the harder road. I have to believe in your ability to see what is in your longer-term interest, and change your behavior to achieve your goals.

Some mortgage companies run a scam to have the borrower make biweekly payments rather than monthly, or thirteen payments per year instead of twelve. They then demonstrate how you will pay off your mortgage in twenty-three years instead of thirty, saving thousands of dollars in interest. The kicker: They often charge a fee to provide this service. And we have already seen the holes in the paying-your-mortgage-early argument.

The Psychology of Debt: What Is It Worth to YOU To Be Debt Free?

Many people, particularly in the frugal Midwest where I am from, have an emotional aversion to debt that supersedes logic. Their psychology is that debt can often destroy dreams.

One of my high school friends, I'll call him John, hired me as his financial advisor. When he was thirty-six years old, he said, "Bruce, I'm going to sell my lake home. I'll walk away with about $200,000 in cash, which is what I owe on my home mortgage. Then I can pay it off and be debt free at age 36. What do you think?"

"John, I wouldn't do that," I told him. I knew his annual income was roughly $300,000, which put him in a combined state and federal tax bracket of about 50 percent. After his mortgage-interest deduction on his taxes, the net cost of his mortgage was just a fraction over 4 percent (this was in the higher mortgage-interest days of the early '90s). I asked, "Don't you think we could invest this $200,000, and do better than 4 percent after taxes?" After John's long pause, he finally said, "Man, that's a great idea! It's so simple! I don't know why I didn't think of it. That's why you're my financial advisor. It's so easy, and so obviously makes sense."

However, after another lengthy pause, John said, "You know, every-thing you said makes sense, but I think I'm going to pay off the mortgage anyway."

He understood the financial logic of my argument in that he could invest that money and earn more than 4 percent after taxes, but the emotional side of his brain, the one that said, "I'm 36 years old—and I'm debt free," won out. Here's the important postscript to the story: Numerous times through the years he has said, "Bruce, I wish I'd listened to you. If I had invested that entire $200,000 back in the early '90s, just look what it'd be worth today based on the stock market we had then."

Fortunately, when John paid off his home mortgage, he began investing each month what he had previously paid on his mortgage, roughly $1,750. So he's still in very, very good shape, but if he had invested the entire $200,000 instead of $1,750 a month, he would have a lot more money today than he does. For him, as well as for many others, the emotion—and the ability to say, "I'm debt free"—was more powerful than the economic logic.

Emotion almost always enters into financial decision-making, for my clients, and for me. Our personalities and experiences condition many of our responses to money, often causing us to take actions that we know intellectually may not be the best. But we choose them anyway because they make us more comfortable emotionally or psychologically.

Ultimately it is not my role to chastise or berate you for your financial behavior. Instead, it's my obligation to educate you so that you will understand why certain choices may or may not be in your best financial interest. Your range of choices is huge for how you will *spend, save, invest, pay taxes, and give away money*—and not one of those choices is always right for every individual. On paper there might be a right answer. In the real world of emotions, personalities, and circumstances, many answers might be appropriate, depending on the individuals.

I am providing you with some tools and insights so that you can better evaluate your options and make your choices, using your money more efficiently to accomplish your goals. Once you understand the fundamentals, you can choose to use or ignore them. This is vastly preferable to listening to conventional wisdom, and then becoming aware days, months, or years later that you had other, better options.

Now, don't go overboard and assume that borrowing money just to invest is a great idea. In fact, that is what you are doing by borrowing money for a mortgage, taking the longest term possible and investing the money that you would be paying each month on a shorter-term mortgage. For most people, borrowing to invest—such as commodity options or margin stock purchases—is usually not a good idea. It's a high-risk use of debt that does not have a place in most investor's portfolios. Investors can make a fortune in a short time, but they can also be wiped out financially if one transaction goes bad.

A Debt Like No Other

I'll explain why it's important not to have "inefficient debt." Inefficient debt is any debt used to fund something that does not have the potential to grow in value or to generate income. This might include personal loans, car loans, and especially credit cards. Also, you receive no tax deduction for interest paid. The real cost for this pre-tax investment requires an after-tax return higher than the interest rate. Reducing this kind of debt should be a high priority due to the high after-tax costs.

On the other hand, "efficient debt" describes any debt that is used to fund something that will benefit your lifestyle, or is a need. This might include a home mortgage or home equity loans. The advantage of efficient debt is that any interest paid is generally tax deductible. It can also create cash flow for other purposes (like paying off inefficient debt).

If you have incurred inefficient debt, one method of eliminating it is to transfer the debt to your home equity. Many people are reluctant to use their home equity to consolidate other debt. This reluctance really stems from a mindset that is behind the times. Certainly, thirty years ago, if people refinanced their home or took out a second mortgage, the neighbors were talking behind their backs about their financial woes. But using your home's equity is economically wise. It provides low interest rates, a tax deduction, and an extended amortization.

In 2007, before the beginning of the economic downturn, real estate values, like the stock market, were at all-time highs. Real estate values had been appreciating by 6 to 9 percent per year for a number of years. Americans felt that their homes were a great place to get money for lifestyle, and they continued to borrow against their equity almost as fast as it was earned. They felt the value of their home would always go up. They were wrong.

As I write this in 2012, the stock market has gained back much of its losses from the fall of 2007 to spring of 2009. But real estate values remain low. Many Americans owe more on their homes than they are currently worth.

I have always been an advocate of using the equity in one's home to enhance overall debt efficiency. If the interest rate can be lowered, and if debt can be amortized over a long period of time, making it tax deductible, and you're borrowing against an appreciating asset, then I believe it may be a good idea. But I have never been an advocate of borrowing against the equity in the home to buy unneeded things or for other investments. And, obviously, since the financial crisis, real estate assets have stopped appreciating the way they used to.

So do not recklessly use this form of debt.

- Defaulting on a mortgage of any kind has greater consequences than defaulting on consumer loans. Mortgage loans are secured by your home, which means that if you can't make payments, you will lose your home. Consumer credit lenders cannot take such drastic risks.

- Avoiding all other kinds of debt, including the high-risk debt of stock-margin purchases and stock and commodity options. Leave those investments to the professional gamblers. Otherwise, buy only what you can pay for with cash.

- Remember that underwriting guidelines have become much tougher since the 2008 recession, so it may be a lot more difficult to get a home equity loan or line of credit.

- Final words on debt.

  - When to use it: rarely.

  - How to use it: to increase your net worth or long-term quality of life, not to buy more things.

After this section called "Spending: What Do You Want, and When Do You Want It?" it is only logical that we summarize with two important questions:

1. How much do you spend? (About money management.)

2. How do you spend it? (About values, need vs. want, and about delayed or instant gratification.)

The answers to both will decide whether you are spending efficiently or incurring inefficient debt.

How much you spend, and how you spend it,
efficiently or inefficiently, will make a big difference
in your overall wealth.

Saving: The Key First Step to Building Wealth

Basically, the three reasons we save are to:

1. Meet emergencies. I recommend that people maintain liquid savings, which means money that is readily accessible in bank accounts or money market funds, to cover six months of basic living expenses,

2. Spend, and

3. Invest.

Saving is quite different from investing, although the two are often confused. We can save without investing, but we usually cannot invest without saving.

Investing presumes that assets have a reasonable expectation of producing earnings or appreciating in value. Most savings accounts, or even many certificates of deposit that pay fixed interest, meet this definition.

Your savings for emergencies and to invest should be, at a minimum, equal to 10 percent (and should be the first 10 percent) of your income. Save first, spend later. Saving for other purposes, such as the new plasma TV or a vacation trip, should be *in addition to* the 10 percent for emergencies and investing. All money you take in should be subject to this 10 percent rule. If you get a gift or a windfall, such as an inheritance, at least 10 percent should go into long-term savings. If you get a raise, increase your savings to match.

Saving for Emergencies

When saving for emergencies, keep up with changes in your own lifestyle. Your $5,000 emergency savings account may have been sufficient when you were in your twenties. But as you age, acquire more obligations, such as children and mortgages, and your income goes up, it may no longer be sufficient. A close look at your potential emergency needs should be part of at least an annual review of your finances. This important concept has become more relevant now, especially because of our recent recession. Many people were very unprepared to be unemployed or under-employed for so long.

Be sure you have enough on hand to cover a medical emergency, a loss of income, or some other catastrophe. Your bills won't stop arriving just because your paychecks do.

The most important factor in deciding which savings vehicles to use for emergency savings is liquidity. Any set-aside emergency funds should be available immediately or within a couple of days. Keep your emergency money separate from your regular checking account so you can't accidentally, or in a moment of weakness, spend it.

The earned rate of return on that money is not nearly as important as your ability to have easy access to it. Some people worry that if their savings are not earning a good rate of return inflation, it will wipe out their purchasing power. They are worrying about the wrong thing. Inflation is a factor in the types of *investments*, but not the type of savings, you choose. If you think there is no difference, read on.

Yearly fluctuations in inflation rates are not a major concern as I work with clients—because there is nothing you can do about inflation. Nearly everything you buy will cost more tomorrow than it does today. Beyond that, we can't predict very far into the future. All we know for sure is that the historical rate of inflation runs about 3 to 4 percent. But that's just a number.

Even government measurements of inflation, such as the Consumer Price Index (CPI), are not relevant to many people. The CPI measures the cost of a "basket" of consumer items, many such items you may never purchase, such as cigarettes, toys, or pet supplies. This is simply a very broad indicator of whether prices are rising at a faster or slower rate, not whether *your* cost of living is increasing by a certain percentage each month or year. Just because the Federal Reserve Board and economists focus their attention on inflation, and every slight change in their opinions invites frenzied analysis, does not mean that it has great significance for you.

One negative result of tremendously expanded coverage of financial markets, such as CNBC on cable TV and MSN Money on the Internet, is that every bit of financial and economic information is treated as important news, and then analyzed to death. This extensive reporting does not make every piece of economic news relevant to most of our lives. Generally, most stories are not really that relevant to the average investor, and the same goes for minor fluctuations in rates of inflation.

Any of your savings with short-term fixed interest rates will barely keep ahead of inflation. But you don't have these savings accounts as investment vehicles. This goes back to the five basic things you can do with money. Two of the five are saving and investing, and they're different.

Instead of worrying about the effect of inflation on your savings, here are two things that will be more productive:

1. Control your spending, and

2. Create an efficient investment strategy.

Investing: Your Progression to Wealth

The goal of investing is quite different from saving. Saving makes money available to you in a secure place, while investing makes that money grow for some future use.

Two rules of thumb:

1. Invest at least 10 percent of your income, and

2. Pay yourself first. Each payday, write your first check to your investment account. Doing so, you'll be able to manage on what remains.

If you instead plan to invest what remains from your paycheck after you've met other needs (and wants), you'll find that most months you have little or nothing left for investing.

The Grand Illusion

This is not where I give you hot stock tips, because searching for outrageous returns is the greatest mistake that most investors make.

Successful investors are not speculators or gamblers, and do not seek to get rich quick through investing. Those who try are deluding themselves, and often end up poorer for the experience.

Step 1: Develop a Strategy

Successful investing does not begin with seeking the next big thing—but with creating a sound strategy for achieving your financial goals.

Successful planning strategies are not usually found by chance. This is not like Columbus setting sail for India, and bumping into America. Investment strategies are constructed with goals and objectives in mind, proper planning, discipline, and the right investment products.

The two great sins of investing are fear and greed. Either one can be your downfall. After the 2008 Wall Street collapse, fear kept many investors out of the market. They've only begun to come back in spring of 2012, thus missing a major run-up in value from late 2011. Greed in the 1990s drove people (who should not have been) to be in the market or in small-cap stocks. After the market losses we saw from 2000 through 2002, and again 2008 to 2009, people have become afraid of the market, and remain on the sidelines. Historically, we've always had market volatility, and we can point to events that created fear or panic, causing people to stay out of the market (See Table 5.3). But investors who remain focused, even during times of war and crisis, have been rewarded with growth to their principal. The greatest value of a good investment strategy is that it will help you overcome any tendencies you may have toward fear or greed. A sound strategy will help you remain patient and confident, and it lets time work for you.

It is possible for most investments to earn a combined return (appreciation plus dividends) of 7 to 9 percent a year. If you earn that consistently over a long period of time, your money will appreciate nicely. Warren Buffet, presently the world's most famous billionaire investor, is well known for his goal of earning annual returns of 8 percent a year. It may not seem much compared to the returns on stocks in the late 1990s, but it sure looks better than the losses many people suffered in the early years of 2000, or the later part of 2008 and early part of 2009.

Here's another hypothetical example to illustrate the value of consistency and stability, over volatility, in your investment portfolio. Table 5.1 compares a steady, modest return to the more volatile returns. Returns of 25 percent a year are very attractive, but come at the risk of seeing significant losses in other years. History proves that 25 percent returns are unsustainable over a long period of time.

Table 5.1.
Stability versus Volatility

	Rate of Return Investment ABC (in %)	Balance	Rate of Return Investment XYZ (in %)	Balance
Initial Amount		$100,000		$100,000
Year 1	7.5	$107,500	25	$125,000
Year 2	7.5	$115,563	25	$156,250
Year 3	7.5	$124,230	20	$187,500
Year 4	7.5	$133,547	20	$225,000
Year 5	7.5	$143,563	-15	$191,250
Year 6	7.5	$154,330	-20	$153,000

A good investment strategy begins by identifying your specific individual goals, and figuring in the time you have to achieve them. Those highly personal decisions, very often driven by your values and what is important to you, will suggest your strategy. Your strategy may include shorter-and longer-term objectives.

1. Are you investing to buy a house, pay for college, or to retire with sufficient income to support your desired lifestyle?

2. How much money will you want for each objective? When will you need it? How can you get there?

3. Will you have to make tradeoffs to achieve those goals? Which take the highest priority? When?

The answers will help you determine your individual strategy, without which it is nearly impossible to know how to invest.

Step 2: Allocate Your Assets

Your values, goals, and individual strategy will determine your asset allocation. Asset allocation determines how much of your money, as a percentage of your total investment, you want to invest in different asset classes. This is the "diversification" you hear so much about. It doesn't mean owning one high-tech stock, one biotech stock, and a handful of shares in General Electric.

Diversification means dividing your portfolio into different types of investments depending on your goals, how long you will hold your investments, and when you may need to withdraw your money.

Creating an investment strategy, building a portfolio, and selecting investments are a lot like building a house. First you determine how much you can spend; next you choose the location and size of house. Then you design just the right number and type of rooms to suit your lifestyle. Only when the house is built do you furnish it to complement everything else.

A portfolio is not just a collection of assets, any more than a house is merely a collection of rooms. If you own a bunch of assets without proper asset allocation, you may, so to speak, have a house with two dining rooms and four living rooms, but no bathrooms or kitchen. Allocating assets is like saying, "I need a house with four bedrooms, one big kitchen, three baths, a living room, and a family room, and here's how big I'd like each of them." Now you've got a functional house—a dwelling that meets your specific needs.

What you have done is allocate space. A portfolio is your allocation of investment space. Instead of doing it by rooms or square footage, you do it by percentages of your resources in asset classes: 10 percent in this type of asset, 40 percent in that, 15 percent in another, and so on.

A proper asset mixture provides an optimal combination of risk and return. And when planning your life and your future, you have to think of risk and return in their broadest terms.

- Risk may not mean losing money; it may mean losing *opportunities*—in financial or personal terms.

- Reward may be more than making money; it may mean increasing financial security or enhancing your enjoyment of life.

The goal is to earn the best return possible over a period of time and in a variety of unpredictable market conditions, rather than to chase the highest possible return at any one given point—and all while minimizing the risk of principal.

Investing should not be a guessing game, at least not if you want to make money consistently. Research demonstrates that market timing and stock selection, combined, account for less than 10 percent of a portfolio's success. The rest is due to asset allocation.

Only after you have determined a strategy and allocated space in your portfolio is it time to consider the merits of specific products. Acquiring those investments is like putting the furniture in each room of your investment house.

Maybe you want:

- A big comfortable overstuffed easy chair in your living room—similar to an annuity or insurance that provides security.

- An entertainment wall in your family room, with all the latest electronic gadgets—like high-flying equities.

- Room in your study for the big oak desk you inherited from your grandfather—like a trust fund for educating your grandchildren.

As with the house and furniture, the options are practically endless. The first requirement is that the asset classes in your portfolio offer everything you've ever wanted, and fit your strategy.

To access the full return potential of the financial markets and reduce risk, portfolios must also be diversified within each asset class. The stock and bond markets are composed of numerous styles and sectors (large value, small growth, international equities, government bonds, corporate bonds, etc.). An efficient management philosophy will have carefully designed strategies for the domestic equity market, international equity market, fixed income market, and so on.

Like the house/real estate analogy, what's most important to remember about investing? Allocation, allocation, allocation.

Three Critical Factors in Asset Allocation

It is easy to allocate space in a house based on the size of your family, your needs, and your lifestyle. But how do you decide to allocate your investments? Financial professionals look at three basic components of each asset class:

1. *Expected rate of return* is simply a historical calculation: how the asset class has performed on average over an extended period of time.

2. *Expected risk level* is a mathematical calculation of the average variance from the expected rate of return. The

greater the average variance, the greater the likelihood that performance will be significantly different from the expected rate of return in any given year.

3. *Expected correlation with other asset classes* is determined by comparing historical performance for various asset classes. As the years pass, we learn that some asset classes tend to perform similarly or quite the opposite of other asset classes.

Rate of Return and Risk Level

Most people get into trouble with investments because they don't know how to balance risk and reward. Successful investing is actually reasonably predictable for those who do it right.

Here I address the rate of return and risk together because they are so closely linked. When you consider the issue logically, risk and return have to be correlated. You wouldn't take a greater risk unless the potential return or reward was also greater. Without greater potential return, why would anyone take the risk?

Read this section carefully if you don't yet appreciate the difference between saving and investing. Many people are afraid of investing, especially in stocks, because of the possible perceived risk of losing some of the principal. Usually I have successfully convinced them that *a greater risk may be they outlive their investments.* (More on this topic later.)

Now I will outline how predictable investments in stocks behave historically. Even if you have already embraced investing in stocks, read on. Many investors are not getting the returns they could, and perhaps should, because they are unwilling to take too much risk, or they do not take a long-enough view of the stock market. In any event, you should find the historical performance of the stock market very interesting, giving you ideas about how to allocate your assets to achieve the goals you have for yourself and those you love.

The Stock Market Benchmark: Remarkable Consistency over Time

The benchmark for many discussions of investment returns is the Standard & Poors (S&P) 500. The S&P 500 is an index that includes the 500 largest companies in the United States (companies are added and removed each year as they grow, shrink, or go out of business). The S&P 500 is widely considered to be a good yardstick for overall stock market performance.

A word of caution. The S&P 500 is an unmanaged index, and you cannot invest directly in that index, although some mutual funds attempt to approximate the performance of the index. The average return does not reflect the impact of any management fees, transaction costs, or expenses. And, of course, past results do not indicate future performance. Also keep in mind that the S&P 500 returns cited are an *average* of 500 companies. An individual company may have fared better or worse in any year or over the course of several years, and therefore the return on investment in its stock may have been better or worse than the average.

Still, it is useful to have some idea of how the broader stock market has done over the years. What's most interesting is that although the average return on the S&P 500 since 1962 is about 9.3 percent for the last fifty years ending in 2011, the range of annual returns from year to year vary greatly from a low of -37 percent recently to a high of 37 percent. (See Table 5.2.)

This historical data is cited to underline what investing truly is: A reasonable expectation that your money may earn money, balancing risk and reward.

Table 5.2

S&P 500 Annual Investment Returns, 1962–2011

Below -20%	-20% to-10%	-10% to 0	0 to 10%	10% to 20%	Over 20%
2008	2001	2000	2011	2010	2009
2002	1993	1990	2007	2006	2003
1974	1966	1981	2005	2004	1999
		1977	1994	1988	1998
		1969	1993	1986	1997
		1962	1992	1979	1996
			1987	1976	1995
			1984	1972	1991
			1978	1971	1989
			1970	1968	1985
				1965	1983
				1964	1982
					1980
					1975
					1967
					1963

Source: Wealth Enhancement Advisory Services, LLC.

Remember that returns on stocks—the most widely used form of investing—do not go in a straight line up or down. The stock market, and therefore investors in stocks, will have some years that are better, or worse, than others. The key is that over longer periods of time, such as the forty-plus years I have used here, stocks show a consistent appreciation as measured by a broad indicator.

This principle will be repeated often: Time is an investor's friend. Over the years the stock market has generally gone up. I have no reason to believe that trend will change over the next ten or twenty or thirty years.

Even in the wake of war, assassination, and other crises, you could have done quite well in the stock market over time, even in the worst of times. If you had invested $10,000 in the S&P 500 Index (remember, though, that such an idea is technically impossible) on the very day of some of the most tragic and horrific events in U.S. history, you still would have enjoyed gains within 10 years—and could have a considerable nest egg by now. (See Table 5.3.) Perhaps Charles Dickens was right: The best of times and the worst of times may occur simultaneously.

Table 5.3
*From Turmoil Comes Opportunity**

	2004 Value	2011 Value
The Great Depression	$ 22,402,098	$ 26,827,453
Pearl Harbor	$ 15,251,892	$ 18,264,781
Cuban Missile Crisis	$ 619,454	$ 741,822
JFK administration	$ 834,352	$ 999,172
Nixon administration	$ 442,561	$ 529,985
Crash of 1987	$ 69,215	$ 82,888
First Gulf War	$ 46,999	$ 56,283
Katrina (August 2005)		$ 11,768
Crash of 2008–09 (March 2009)		$ 18,151

*These are hypothetical examples for illustrative purposes only.
Source: Wealth Enhancement Advisory Services, LLC.

Despite the disclaimers, investing in stocks provides that "reasonable" expectation long term. Of course, no well-planned portfolio will ever be made up *entirely* of investments in stocks. Proper asset allocation has the capability to enhance returns, and reduce risk. Done properly, asset allocation levels out the highs and lows of equity investing, making investing more a train ride through gently rolling foothills instead of the steep climbs and hair-raising, zero-gravity drops of a roller coaster.

Most Americans' primary investment objective is to provide for their retirement.

Inflation is not a major concern with your savings, but with investing, it takes on greater importance. American males' life expectancy is reaching 75.7 years, and American females, 80.8. Thus, many people will be living off their retirement investments for nearly half as long as it took them to accumulate the money to invest for retirement. The big question is, will you outlive your investments? Will you have enough money to live the lifestyle you want? Inflation will likely play a big part in how you ultimately answer that question.

Once again, don't worry about monthly or yearly changes in the inflation rate. Even for investment purposes, those fluctuations have little importance. What matters is that over many years, the rate of inflation has remained consistently at 3 to 4 percent on average. You can use this number with some confidence in any financial plan.

The greatest impact of inflation on investing is that it can turn "low-risk" investments into "high-risk" investments. Many people like to invest in what they consider "low-risk" investments, such as certificates of deposit (CDs), savings accounts, money markets, and other fixed-interest investments. These vehicles provide ways to protect your principal—but for many that's not enough. If your nest egg doesn't grow faster than your cost of living, your purchasing power actually steadily decreases, and it will have a detrimental impact on your lifestyle, especially if you're retired, and your only source of income is your investments.

To keep inflation from reducing a nest egg to near nothing, most people probably need to allocate at least some portion of their investment assets into something that has the opportunity to beat inflation. Low-risk investment vehicles play a role in a well-diversified portfolio or asset allocation, but low-risk investments alone may not provide the investment returns that one needs to keep up with inflation. The likeliest way for most people to be able to keep up with inflation is by having some part of their investment allocation in equities or stocks.

History proves that equities provide an effective means to outpace inflation.

Fixed-Interest Investments: Security and Protection of Principal

Fixed-interest investments are more appropriate for saving than investing, yet most brokerages advise their clients to maintain an asset allocation of, say, 50 percent stocks, 30 percent bonds, and 20 percent cash, to give but one example. Are they wrong? No. Fixed-interest investments, such as bonds, are an important asset class that should be part of most portfolios because they often provide "negative correlation" (we'll get to that concept) with equity or stock investments. For instance in 2008, the S&P 500 index declined 37 percent while bonds increased in value by 5.2 percent. In this instance there was negative correlation. As stock prices dropped, bond prices rose. Within investment portfolios, that increase in the value of bonds helped offset the decline in stock prices.

What's my opposition to fixed-interest investments? It's when they comprise all or too much of someone's portfolio. As an intricate part of a portfolio, they are essential. As a substitute for an investment strategy, they are sadly and perhaps dangerously inefficient.

Final Words on Risk

How do you know if any of the fixed-interest investments I've described are appropriate for you? Which asset allocation you can live with should be determined by your personal tolerance for risk, as well as your values and goals. If you lie awake worrying about your investments, you should probably invest your money in vehicles that are less risky. Don't forget, however, that the risk of outliving your money is a much scarier risk than making some investments that could, in the worst case, lose money, but on average should provide better returns.

My primary duty as a financial advisor is to educate people about the true risks of investing—or not investing at all. To put it simply, even for the most risk-averse people, risk tolerance increases with greater knowledge of investment options and strategies.

One way to help you strike the balance between risk and reward is to look more closely at how various assets perform relative to others.

It's time to examine the third important element of asset allocation: the correlation of each asset's historical performance.

Correlation: A Negative Is Positive

If we fill our portfolio with only asset classes that tend to perform alike, we maximize our risk. If market and economic conditions favor those asset classes, we could do very well. But if any of those asset classes performs badly, they probably will all go into the tank. The much-smarter option is to balance asset classes, finding the best combination of asset classes to get optimum performance while minimizing volatility.

Even if one asset class tends to be very risky, meaning that it can fluctuate wildly over the years, we can balance that asset class with another that also appears risky, but tends to move in the opposite direction. That balance reduces the risk in our portfolio and increases the returns over time. That's an example of negative correlation, which is positive in asset allocation. Ideally, the asset classes you choose will have this "negative" correlation built in.

A Love Story: The Sunny Shores of Rainy Lake

To put negative correlation in simple terms, consider this love story. A young woman opened a resort on beautiful Rainy Lake in northern Minnesota. She was a smart businessperson, and her guests adored her. Her problem was that her business depended on the weather. In a hot, sunny summer, she made a 50 percent return on her investment. But in cold, damp summers, she would typically lose 25 percent. The ups and downs were a little unsettling for her.

As luck would have it, however, a regular guest at her resort was a bachelor who owned an umbrella company. His business had the opposite problem: In clear, sunny weather, he lost 25 percent, but when the weather was blustery and wet, he enjoyed a hefty 50 percent return on his investment.

Perhaps it was inevitable that the resort owner and the umbrella maker would fall in love, get married, and pool their assets. Now neither of them worries about the weather because, rain or shine, they make a nice, steady 12.5 percent on their combined investments.

That is negative correlation—and it's the objective of asset allocation, as well as diversification within a portfolio. This story is clearly an oversimplification to make a point, but my money management philosophy is very simple. With a well-diversified, actively managed portfolio, we reduce performance peaks and valleys, and achieve competitive long-term performance with less risk.

Of course, if the resort owner and umbrella maker were extremely good at guessing which summers would be sunny and which would be rainy, they could take full advantage of both conditions, shifting their assets as appropriate, and really make a killing. But anyone who could predict whether a summer will be bright and warm, or cold and damp, would have a gift they could use to such financial advantage that they wouldn't need advice from me on how to create wealth.

Guessing the ups and downs of the stock market is a bit like predicting the weather. Not even the professionals are right all the time—in weather or stocks—and they're smart enough to know it. So they minimize their risk and maximize the potential for return by using percentages. The meteorologist says we have a 60 percent chance of rain. The money manager says we have 60 percent of our portfolio in stocks, 30 percent in bonds, and 10 percent in cash.

Your individual circumstances will determine how you should allocate your assets. People with a longer timeline, like a thirty-year-old, are probably best off significantly invested in equities. Over the length of time that they are likely to be invested, stocks will almost certainly outperform all other asset classes. As people get older, their asset allocation should weigh two factors: 1) their dependence on income from their investments, and 2) the amount of their debt.

- Those with a higher net worth as well as low or no debt will likely want to remain fully invested in stocks, or maintain a high percentage of their portfolio in equities.

- Those who will need to depend on their investment returns for living expenses will likely want to choose a different mixture of assets, keeping in mind that a "safe" strategy isn't safe if it exposes you to the risk of running out of money.

When You Can't Resist Speculating

For many people picking stocks is like a game, hobby, or avocation, in that every morning they check the newspaper or Internet to see how they've done. If you insist on "scratching that itch," set aside a small percentage—not more than 10 percent—of your portfolio to invest in individual speculative stocks. It's fun to play around with, and you get a chance once in a while to pick a stock that can appreciate more dramatically than most assets in your investment portfolio. But don't rely on these investments to provide for your retirement or your children's education. If one of my picks does well, I put the profits back into my general portfolio and maintain my asset allocation.

Step 3: Select Your Investments

After you have established a strategy based on where you want to go, and determined the ideal asset allocation to get you there, the next step is to select individual investments within your portfolio. As you build your portfolio, you determine which investments in each asset class will give you the ideal mixture of assets to reduce risk and enhance return.

Finally, you are ready to select individual investments. Most investors want to jump straight to selecting investments, but that really must come after a great deal of planning and careful consideration.

Within each asset class, you want to pursue competitive returns for that particular asset class that gives you diversification and negative correlation. Then find specific investments that provide returns equal-to or better-than-the-average within that class. But be sure you are comparing apples to apples. Don't compare returns in one asset class with those of another. If you do, you will be tempted to throw out your strategy and just chase the highest returns, which means you may in turn be chased by the highest risk.

Stick to your plan, and accept the best returns you can get in a balanced portfolio.

Equity Investing: Appreciation, Growth of Principal

You should be well aware of the risks of investing in stocks, and I've already told you about the consistency of historical returns over several years. But before you begin selecting stocks to meet your asset allocation criteria, you need to consider more than market risk— specifically the risk that your stocks will decline in value. Also keep in mind the following risks inherent in equity investing:

- Currency risk. This is the risk that the value of currencies will fluctuate widely. For example, if the euro declines against the U.S. dollar, and you own a European stock fund, the euro, when translated back into dollars, could have a negative impact on fund performance.

- Economic risk. This is risk associated with economic uncertainty. For example, the recent U.S. economic downturn had a dire effect on many cyclical businesses, such as airlines and steel, where earnings fell below levels of prior years.

- Financial credit risk. Inherent in all business is the uncertainty of the future of the corporation issuing a security. For example, if a company finds itself in financial straits, it may not be able to meet its payments to its bondholders.

- Inflation risk. This risk is the danger that rising prices will cut into a company's margins. Do they have pricing power— the ability to raise their prices as the cost of their materials increases? This is especially true of companies that rely heavily on a single commodity. Airlines, for instance, are impacted greatly by changes in oil prices, which hit all-time highs in 2004.

- Interest rate risk. Changes in interest rates may hurt a company's performance. Do they need to go to credit markets often for working capital? Does the company need to borrow money regularly to build or update new facilities?

- Management risk. This risk relates to the quality and stability of a corporation's management, and its impact on business and security prices. For example, poor management choices can have an effect on the company's underlying security or share prices.

The Most Common Method of Stock Ownership: Mutual Funds

Many people invest in equities primarily through mutual funds, a much easier way to diversify your portfolio than buying all the stocks yourself. Very few people actually have the assets to diversify strictly through ownership of individual stocks. Mutual funds, therefore, should be a significant part of almost every portfolio.

One of the basic decisions facing many fund investors is whether to buy a load fund or a no-load fund. A load fund has a sales charge that is paid either at the time of investment or withdrawal; thus the terms "front load" and "back load." Many investment advisors discourage people from buying load funds, but I'm not so quick to disqualify them.

I recommend mutual funds that I think will provide the greatest net return in their asset class. I do not disqualify a fund because it has a load, or sales commission, if it provides the likelihood of superior performance. That said, I recommend load funds only for longer-term investments. In the shorter term, the load may dilute the net return on your investment. Over the years, however, some load funds may be worth it. I would recommend no-load funds, for example, if you have a teenager who is saving for college. Because you'll need the money in three or four years, a no-load fund makes more sense. Anytime you anticipate redeeming shares within a few years, look at no-load funds.

If you plan to leave the money invested for a longer time, find the best fund, regardless of "load."

What should people do with underperforming mutual funds? It's hard to give one simple answer because to give good advice, I need to know more. For instance:

- Is the fund performing poorly against the market as a whole?

- Or is it underperforming similar funds?

- Does the fund represent an asset class that you want in your portfolio?

- Does it provide the asset allocation your strategy dictates?

How long you hold underperforming funds depends on why you bought them, how they fit with your overall goals and values, and where they fit in your overall strategy. If you carefully selected funds to provide good asset allocation, be patient, with a few caveats.

Compare your fund's performance with others in the same asset class, such as large-cap growth, international, or small-cap value.

- If your funds consistently underperform similar funds that buy the same type of assets and have the same investment philosophy, then you might consider changing funds.

- If your funds are not performing well, but neither are others in that asset class, and it's an asset class you want in your portfolio, hang on to them.

Step 4: Manage Your Investments

You are not done yet. You have a brilliant strategy in place, asset classes that suit your personal goals and values to a T, a portfolio you are quite sure will enhance your returns over many years, and carefully researched investments within your chosen asset classes. Now you sit back and watch your portfolio grow, right? Investing doesn't work that way. Perhaps the hardest work is done, but successful investors never just walk away and let their investments manage themselves. If not tended to, portfolios have a bad habit of going seriously off course.

Any investment plan requires continuous management to achieve long-term success.

Continuous Management and Rebalancing

Your asset allocation was just right when you started your investment plan, but what happens after six months or a year? Your goal was to balance asset classes that tend to perform differently as a group, so if one performs poorly, the others are likely to perform better. Over a period of time, that should increase average returns. But if one asset class performs better than others, it changes the percentage of your investment in each. The time has come to rebalance your portfolio.

Rebalancing means buying and selling assets to bring the percentages of assets within your portfolio back in line with your asset-allocation strategy. However, rebalancing your portfolio to maintain your asset allocation can be complicated, especially in taxable accounts. Capital-gains taxes, surrender charges, and back-end loads on mutual funds may make rebalancing too expensive to do quarterly. If this is the case, it's still in your interest to rebalance your account at least annually, even if you incur some costs. Of course, if your assets are in tax-deferred plans (IRAs, 401(k)s), you don't have to worry about capital gains. The ease of rebalancing is one advantage of variable annuities and variable universal life insurance; those products usually make it easy to transfer money at no cost from one subaccount to another within the plan.

Because I consider asset allocation and, therefore, rebalancing, the linchpins of successful investing, I want to present three strategies to hypothetically illustrate the concepts. For our purposes, we'll choose two imaginary mutual funds, one a "large cap" fund and another a "small cap" fund. We'll start with $10,000 in each, because that represents a rudimentary form of asset allocation, and see what happens.

Let's say that in the first year, the large cap fund doubles in value, and the small cap fund loses half its value. Clearly, those are extreme returns used to make a point. Few funds will double in value or lose half their value in a year, although both extremes have actually occurred in the last decade. Then, for the purposes of comparing strategies, we'll say that the funds reverse performance the second year: The small cap fund doubles in value, and the large cap fund loses half its value.

Strategy #1: Buy and Hold

The first strategy, if we can call it that, is to "buy and hold." You'll hear many investment advisors and TV's financial talking heads recommend that you buy a stock or mutual fund, put it away, and then ignore it. That may be a fine idea if you're looking at an isolated equity investment. Are you convinced now that looking at any investment outside of your overall portfolio is not a good idea? Table 5.4 indicates what happens to our investments if we buy and hold—in other words, if we do nothing to manage our investments.

Table 5.4.
Your Investment When You Buy and Hold

	Large Cap Fund	Small Cap Fund	Total Value	Return (in%)
Investment	$10,000	$10,000	$20,000	
1st year return	-50%	100%		
Value	$5,000	$20,000	$25,000	25
Hold	$5,000	$20,000		
2nd year return	100%	-50%		
Value	$10,000	$10,000	$20,000	0

The problem with buying and holding is that it does not maintain an optimal asset allocation. Investments that perform well become a larger percentage of your portfolio. In this example, after the first year, clearly your asset allocation is skewed. You now have only 20 percent of your assets in large cap and 80 percent in small cap investments. That is not the asset allocation you chose at the start, so why would you accept that asset allocation after one year? Your approach is out of whack if you follow a buy-and-hold strategy instead of rebalancing. The portfolios of people who follow this course can become over-weighted in a few asset classes. If the market turns against those asset classes, those portfolios can go downhill fast. It is much better to manage your portfolio continuously with regular rebalancing to maintain the desired asset allocation.

Strategy # 2: Chase the Hot Fund

The second option is to chase the hot fund. I hesitate to call it a strategy because in this example, emotions have taken control of investing. Unfortunately, this is typical investing behavior. You think that because the value fund is doing so well, you should put all of your money into that fund. Table 5.5 illustrates what happens if you do.

Table 5.5.
Your Investment When You Chase the Hot Fund

	Large Cap Fund	Small Cap Fund	Total Value	Return (in%)
Investment	$10,000	$10,000	$20,000	
1st year return	-50%	100%		
Value	$5,000	$20,000	$25,000	25
Chase	$-5,000	$+5,000		
Value	$0	$25,000		
2nd year return	100%	-50%		
Value	$0	$12,500	$12,500	-37.5

What this decision represents is complete abandonment of your asset allocation, and in this hypothetical example, it would cost you. Too many people try too hard to figure out when to get into and out of markets.

The 2012 Quantitative Analysis of Investor Behavior conducted by DALBAR® shows that the average equity investor underperformed the S&P 500 by 4.32 percent for the past twenty years on an annualized basis, and 7.85 percent for 2011. Over the long and short term, individuals have demonstrated that irrational decisions lead to inferior returns.

This means that the average investor had a return of 3.49 percent over a twenty-year period and a negative 5.73 percent for the past twelve months in the same time period that the S&P 500 was appreciating in value, up 7.81 percent over twenty years and 2.12 percent for 2011. How could that be? Because investors jumped on board when the market is doing well, and then got out of the market when they were doing badly. Hot funds had attracted investors, but when the funds cooled off, investors abandoned them for other hot funds. The investors in those funds, on average, were buying high and selling low, exactly the opposite of every investor's intention.

Strategy #3: Rebalance

As Table 5.6 illustrates, the third and best option is to rebalance the portfolio after the first year, bringing your asset allocation back in line with what you wanted from the start, namely, 50 percent in each type of fund.

Table 5.6.
The Benefits of Rebalancing

	Large Cap Fund	Small Cap Fund	Total Value	Return (in%)
Investment	$10,000	$10,000	$20,000	
1st year return	-50%	100%		
Value	$5,000	$20,000	$25,000	25
Rebalance	$12,500	$12,500		
2nd year return	100%	-50%		
Value	$25,000	$6,250	$31,250	56.25

The hypothetical returns in this example have been exaggerated to make a point. In reality, there is no way to predict returns, and the differences in the strategies are likely to be less dramatic than shown here. Do you see the point? If you maintain the asset allocation you deem optimal, by rebalancing your portfolio regularly, you are less likely to fall victim to the shifts in market sentiment and to wild swings in performance. Keep this in mind:

Our objective is to achieve optimal long-term performance rather than pursue the highest possible returns at any one point in time. Rebalancing is an essential component of long-term success.

Rebalancing Applies Across the Board

Rebalancing applies to your entire portfolio of investments, whatever that may be, whether stocks, bonds, real estate, or other investments. I used mutual funds to demonstrate rebalancing in the preceding example, largely because they are the most common form of equity investing. Investors achieve diversification much more easily through mutual funds than they can through owning individual stocks.

Caution: Rebalancing mutual funds requires an additional step. Monitor your funds to be sure that they are giving you the asset allocation you thought you were getting. In the competition for investors, fund managers are tempted to fudge their investment discipline a bit in pursuit of stocks that are hot, even if they are slightly outside the stated investment "style" of the fund. This "style drift" is very common. Be sure to monitor your fund's buy-and-sell decisions to ensure that they are not drifting into asset classes that don't meet your asset allocation target. If a fund begins to invest in assets outside its professed targets, your asset allocation may be skewed.

- Example: You choose to allocate some of your investments to a "value" mutual fund that invests in companies that are considered undervalued. But then you learn that the fund managers have begun to invest in some faster "growth" companies to improve their returns. That should not please you if you chose that fund precisely because it did not invest in faster-growth companies, which are often more volatile. You may already own shares in another fund that has growth as its stated objective. Now you have more of your assets than you might have wanted invested in "growth" companies. During your annual rebalancing, you may want to shift your funds allocated to "value" investments to another value fund that has maintained its discipline.

The only way to check for this style drift is to carefully read the reports that your fund sends you. You need to examine closely the type of stocks the fund holds to be sure that they are staying true to their goals

Timing Your Investments

In these days of detailed and ubiquitous reporting on stock markets, one of the great dangers facing individual investors is the temptation to time the market. Never forget that *time, not timing,* is the investor's greatest ally.

If your biggest concern is *when* to invest your money, you're worrying about the wrong thing. Investing a set amount each month is fine as a *saving* strategy, but as an *investing* strategy, it's flawed. The best time to invest is as soon as you can. If you have created your asset allocation strategy, invest now.

But many people don't follow this advice, or they try to beat the market by picking the right time to invest. The two most popular methods of trying to beat the market that way are dollar cost averaging and market timing.

Dollar Cost Averaging Is Overrated

Many investment advisors suggest that one way to get the best of all worlds in investing is to "dollar cost average" your investment. Dollar cost averaging is an excellent way to invest regularly. It requires you to set aside money each month for investing. But I do not recommend dollar cost averaging if you have a lump sum of money to invest. In most cases, the sooner you invest, the better.

Dollar cost averaging is a nugget of misguided "wisdom" that seems to be promoted primarily by mutual fund companies—although it has its advocates among those whose financial "qualification" is limited to their ability to read the financial news on TV.

In dollar cost averaging, rather than investing money in stocks or mutual funds in one lump sum, you invest a set amount of money every month. The thinking is that since the dollar amount remains consistent, the investor acquires more shares when prices are low, and fewer when share prices are high. The supposed advantage is that the average price the consumer pays is less than the average price at which the security is offered.[2]

Here's how dollar cost averaging works:

- In successive months we invest $100 into a mutual fund.

- The first month the share price is $10. Therefore, we buy 10 shares.

- The second month, the share price is only $5. Consequently, we buy 20 shares.

- To calculate the average share price of the fund at the time we made our purchases, we add the prices the fund was offered at, and divide by the number of purchases ($10 + $5 ÷ 2 = $7.5).

- The average share price is $7.50. However, we spent $200 to acquire 30 shares, meaning our average worth of each share is only $6.67 ($200 ÷ 30).

That seems like a pretty good deal—if that's as far as you care to go in analyzing your costs. But the fact remains that your thirty shares are not worth $6.67 a share; they are now worth only $5 each. If the share price then bounces back up, your purchase at $5 a share will look good. But what if it goes down further? Wouldn't you have been better off to have just kept your money in the bank until you *knew* share prices would go up? But if you did know the price would go up from $5, why did you buy only twenty shares at that price?

Conversely, what if the original share price increased by 50 percent from one month to the next, instead of decreasing by that amount— and continued to go up every month after that? Then dollar cost averaging wouldn't look so good, either. If you had had the money to

---

2. Periodic investment plans do not assure a profit or protect against loss in a declining market. Dollar-cost averaging involves continuous investment in securities regardless of the fluctuating price of such securities. Investors should carefully consider their ability to continue their investments during periods of low price levels.

invest, you would have been far better off investing it all at the beginning.

The people who recommend dollar cost averaging say, "You don't know what the market will do, and you're crazy to guess, so hedge your bets by investing a little at a time. You won't miss out on long rallies or get hurt as badly by a big crash."

It is true that markets are as likely to go up as down on any given day, but we do know that over a period of time, markets have generally gone up. Although, again, past performance does not guarantee future results, the average annual increase for the S&P 500 historically is nearly 9 percent. It seems that if you really want to play the law of averages, you would want your money in the market sooner rather than later.

Although the popular perception of markets is that they increase steadily, but plummet suddenly, research provides an interesting counterpoint. The most precipitous collapses of markets have occurred on single infamous days such as Black Monday in 1929 and Black Tuesday in 1987. But research demonstrates that one-day rallies can also have an enormous impact on overall performance.

If you take just the best thirty days away from the 2,500-plus trading days in the ten-year period from 2002 to 2011, the average annual return drops—from 0.92 percent to negative 13.59 percent per year. (See Table 5.7.) That's if you missed, on average, only three trading days a year for that ten-year period. Investors who dollar cost average are going to miss some of these big up days, too, just as they avoid some of the big down days. Dollar cost averaging is guessing with a hedge, but with no real rationale for the guessing. Perhaps a consistent investment plan such as dollar cost averaging gives some people the illusion of an investment strategy where none really exists.

Table 5.7
Don't Miss The Good Days

	S&P 500 Annualized Returns (in%)
1/1/2002–12/31/2011 (2,520 trading days)	0.92%
Minus the 10 best days	-5.88%
Minus the 20 best days	-10.04%
Minus the 30 best days	-13.59%

Source: Wealth Enhancement Advisory Services, LLC. The S&P 500 is an unmanaged index; investors cannot invest directly in an index.
Remember: Past performance does not guarantee future results.

So why do people recommend dollar cost averaging as an investment strategy? Mutual fund companies stand to gain the most if you follow the strategy. Of course, it would be in their interest, too, if you invested as much as you could with them as soon as you could. But a fund company also wants you to become a regular investor. They want you to get in the habit of adding to your account every month, and they don't want you to be scared off by a little downturn in the market.

Dollar cost averaging is a wonderful way to keep people invested even if markets are down for a time. It's a theory that encourages people to look at the bright side of bad markets: "Wow, look how cheaply I'm buying shares this month."

Perhaps people who dollar cost average are less likely to withdraw their money from funds when stocks plunge or those funds perform poorly.

Redemptions can get very expensive for those mutual funds if enough shareholders redeem their shares at the same time. If mutual funds do not have enough cash reserves to pay off redemptions, they have to sell assets—and being forced to sell assets when prices are low is not very good for overall performance. Mutual funds are more profitable for their managers if people invest steadily and consistently over a long period of time, instead of jumping into and out of the funds, even with larger sums.

Dollar cost averaging is a defensive strategy—a saving strategy—not an efficiency strategy.

It is for *accumulating* assets, not *allocating* assets already accumulated. It has the potential to work fine for saving $50, $100, or $200 a month—and if you don't have any investments or savings, start doing that. But if you already have $5,000, $10,000, or even $20,000 available, it is more efficient to invest that money in one lump sum as soon as possible, properly allocated, of course.

Overthinking and Underperforming

Market timing: Putting money into or pulling it out of stocks based on whether one thinks the market is going up or down in the short term or even on a given day—or hour!

Market timing is the more aggressive method of trying to outguess the market that doesn't even present the illusion of strategy—it's pure gambling.

Those who reduce investing to guessing market moves are making investing far more complicated and potentially far less rewarding than it should be. We all know someone who has picked the right time to make an investment, and gloated, "I bought the sucker and it went up 30 percent the next week." They probably mention it only because it was such a rarity in their investment experience. Most of us know very few people, if any, who have consistently picked the right time to make an investment. It's tough to replicate good luck, and know when those three big days each year are going to fall.

If market timing were really so simple that your uncle Wilbur could master it, don't you think some Wall Street company with millions to spend on computer software and mathematicians would eventually also figure it out? Well, they haven't, and many high-flying companies and stock pickers have had their comeuppance in bankruptcy court when their theories crashed, along with their portfolios.

What Are You Waiting For, Investor?

In February 2009, I had a client couple with a long time horizon that refused to invest in the stock market because of recent declines. Despite my encouragement and sharing of long-term historical data about the stock market, this couple was convinced that they should wait until the market "stabilized." Finally, over one year later, they came back in and implemented our recommendations, which included investing in the stock market. But what was their cost of waiting? The market in the one year from March 1, 2009, to February 28, 2010, as measured by the S&P 500, went up 53.6 percent

If you were confident that buying something for $100 was a good purchase, but then you saw it on sale for $60, would you refuse to buy it just because the price had dropped? Of course not. You can't get out your checkbook fast enough. Conversely, if instead of going on sale, the item's price was raised to $140, would you think, "It's even more valuable now, so it's an even better buy"? Stocks are the only purchase that I can think of that people react to this irrationally.

Unfortunately, when it comes to investments, most people respond and react emotionally, not logically.

One of the greatest benefits of a good financial plan is that it gives you something concrete to cling to when your emotions are about to carry you away. A classic movie, *Casablanca,* gave us a timeless song that contains a line all investors should keep in mind. Play it, Sam: "You must remember this, a kiss is still a kiss, a sigh is just a sigh, the fundamental things apply as time goes by."

No obvious changes in the fundamentals of investing and markets came out of the supercharged markets of the 1990s, even though the decade did give us an unprecedented bull market. That was followed by three years of terrible equity performance, but pretty good returns on bonds. Anything is possible in financial markets. Some people think that the fundamentals have changed, first for the best, then for the worst. I doubt that opinions on either extreme will be correct. I think the fundamental things apply—and will continue to for years.

Although there is no guarantee, it's possible the average annual returns on money invested in equities will remain not too far from the historical average of about 8 percent. At some point, we will certainly have a couple of years of lower returns and slower growth, followed by some good years. The investors who have no strategy, but just chase hot stocks, will be hurt the worst. Investors who have proper asset allocation in their portfolios will have the potential to see a return on their investments that could exceed what they would be getting if they were totally invested in fixed-rate investments. Your asset allocation may give a prominent place to equity investments, but it will also balance those investments with others that are expected to have a lower correlation.

Many in the financial industry encourage dollar cost averaging because it commits people to investing money regularly and trading more often, which can generate commissions. But what may be good for them is not necessarily good for you. Invest regularly, but if you have more to invest than usual, don't hold some of it back to dollar cost average. Don't succumb to the siren song of whatever is hot at the moment.

Put your money to work for you as soon as you can, but be sure to follow your investment strategy.

Here's a personal anecdote about time—not timing—in terms of stock market investments. My wife and I got married in June of 1987. Shortly after, I received a bonus at the job I had at that time. Times were tight. Month to month we wondered if we were going to have rent money. My wife wanted to have that bonus money more accessible in the bank. But I pointed out that I felt it would perform better in the stock market, and would still be accessible if we really needed it. We decided to put roughly $10,000 into a mutual fund. (It was one of the few times in our nearly twenty-five years of marriage that I actually won the debate.)

Shortly after we invested this money, the Dow took a big hit on October 19, 1987. Our mutual fund fell from $10,000 to just under $6,000, a whopping decrease of more than 40 percent. The question was: What should we do now? Should we take our $6,000 and put it in a bank? That's what my wife wanted to do, but we didn't. If we had done that, and averaged a 6 percent annual return over fifteen years, it would have accrued to roughly $15,000. We could have waited until we had some recovery in the market, and gained back what we lost, and got back to $10,000—and then put that in a CD at 6 percent. If so, today we would have a little more than $20,000. We didn't do that, either. We assumed it would be a long-term investment, and we would only tap it in the short term if we were desperate. We sat tight and held on, and the mutual fund is now worth more than $60,000.

The moral of the story: The equity investment, the mutual fund, over time significantly outperformed the fixed-interest alternative investments, although one could argue that we incurred a higher degree of risk. But, as I have noted, there is more than one way to measure risk.

Start Investing Early

No time is better than right now to start any investment plan. Time is your greatest ally, and the longer you invest, the better off you will be.

Let's assume that Jill, at age twenty-one, starts to put $5,000 per year into a Roth IRA with no income tax consequences whatsoever. She does this for only ten years—and at age thirty, she stops. Why doesn't really matter. Let's assume that her account can earn 8 percent each and every year. The account continues to accrue until she's sixty-five. The total value of her account at age sixty-five, earning 8 percent every year, would be $1,156,620. (See Table 5.8.)

Now, her identical twin, Jack, doesn't start to fund his Roth IRA until he's thirty-one. Jack also puts away $5,000 per year, in the same investment Jill does, and earns the same 8 percent each and every year. Furthermore, Jack makes these contributions for thirty-five years—from thirty-one until sixty-five.

- Jack's total amount of contributions is $175,000 over a thirty-five-year period of time.

- Jill's total contribution was $50,000 over a ten-year period.

- Jack invested $125,000 more than Jill, but he started ten years later.

- Jack's account at age sixty-five accrues to $930,511, or $226,109 less than Jill's.

The moral of the story: Start investing as soon as you can, as much as you can, as consistently as you can. Don't wait. Pay yourself first and you may be rewarded long-term. There is a huge cost in waiting.

Table 5.8.
The Benefits of Investing Early
Note: Assumes that contributions are made in January; also assumes 8 percent growth annually.

Age	Beginning of Year Value	Jill's Annual Contributions	End of Year 8% Growth	Age	Beginning of Year Value	Jack's Annual Contributions	End of Year 8% Growth
21	0	5,000	5,400	21	0	0	0
22	5,400	5,000	11,232	22	0	0	0
23	11,232	5,000	17,531	23	0	0	0
24	17,531	5,000	24,333	24	0	0	0
25	24,333	5,000	31,680	25	0	0	0
26	31,680	5,000	39,614	26	0	0	0
27	39,614	5,000	48,183	27	0	0	0
28	48,183	5,000	57,438	28	0	0	0
29	57,438	5,000	67,433	29	0	0	0
30	67,433	5,000	78,227	30	0	0	0
31	78,227	0	84,486	31	0	5,000	5,400
32	84,486	0	91,244	32	5,400	5,000	11,232
33	91,244	0	98,544	33	11,232	5,000	17,531
34	98,544	0	106,428	34	17,531	5,000	24,333
35	106,428	0	114,942	35	24,333	5,000	31,680
36	114,942	0	124,137	36	31,680	5,000	39,614
37	124,137	0	134,068	37	39,614	5,000	48,183
38	134,068	0	144,794	38	48,183	5,000	57,438
39	144,794	0	156,377	39	57,438	5,000	67,433
40	156,377	0	168,887	40	67,433	5,000	78,227
41	168,887	0	182,398	41	78,227	5,000	89,886
42	182,398	0	196,990	42	89,886	5,000	102,476
43	196,990	0	212,749	43	102,476	5,000	116,075
44	212,749	0	229,769	44	116,075	5,000	130,761
45	229,769	0	248,151	45	130,761	5,000	146,621
46	248,151	0	268,003	46	146,621	5,000	163,751
47	268,003	0	289,443	47	163,751	5,000	182,251
48	289,443	0	312,598	48	182,251	5,000	202,231
49	312,598	0	337,606	49	202,231	5,000	223,810
50	337,606	0	364,615	50	223,810	5,000	247,115

Age	Beginning of Year Value	Jill's Annual Contributions	End of Year 8% Growth	Age	Beginning of Year Value	Jack's Annual Contributions	End of Year 8% Growth
51	364,615	0	393,784	51	247,115	5,000	272,284
52	393,784	0	425,287	52	272,284	5,000	299,466
53	425,287	0	459,310	53	299,466	5,000	328,824
54	459,310	0	496,054	54	328,824	5,000	360,530
55	496,054	0	535,739	55	360,530	5,000	394,772
56	535,739	0	578,598	56	394,772	5,000	431,754
57	578,598	0	624,886	57	431,754	5,000	471,694
58	624,886	0	674,876	58	471,694	5,000	514,830
59	674,876	0	728,867	59	514,830	5,000	561,416
60	728,867	0	787,176	60	561,416	5,000	611,729
61	787,176	0	850,150	61	611,729	5,000	666,068
62	850,150	0	918,162	62	666,068	5,000	724,753
63	918,162	0	991,615	63	724,753	5,000	788,133
64	991,615	0	1,070,944	64	788,133	5,000	856,584
65	1,070,944	0	1,156,620	65	856,584	5,000	930,511

Timing Your Withdrawals or Adjustments to Your Portfolio

One of the great investing mistakes is that people plan only for the accumulation of investment assets, but not for the distribution of investment assets. This also has a huge impact on your strategy and the timing of your investment. (See "Planning for Retirement" in chapter 1 for more detail.)

As a general rule, I recommend that anytime you are within five years of needing to use the money in your investment accounts, shift your money into more conservative, lower-risk asset classes. Does this contradict my argument that exposure to stocks is necessary for most people? Not at all. I already stated that over longer periods of time, such as ten years, stock markets have usually outperformed fixed-interest investments, and given some time, generally do better. But equities are subject to greater fluctuation in shorter periods of time. Inevitably stock markets do go through good and bad years. Some years, equities most likely will lose money. If you don't have the time to wait out those dips in the market, they can pose more risk than I think is acceptable. My advice to anyone who intends to spend money in an investment account within five years would be to shift at least some, if not all, of that money into assets that will not depreciate.

This applies to investing for almost any purpose. If you're investing to pay for college for your child, when your child reaches high school, you should shift your investments into more conservative vehicles. If you intend to retire within five years, and you will need income from your investments to pay living expenses, you should begin to shift some of your investments. The mistake many people make, however, is shifting into more conservative investments before they should.

- Example: You are age fifty-five, and plan to retire in ten years. You have 50 percent of your retirement investments in aggressive mutual funds. Is that too much? For many people in that situation, 50 percent of their equity investment in aggressive funds would not be too much—if they are allocated appropriately. Why? Because those funds have the greatest potential for appreciation, and people of that age still have a long time horizon. Markets have ups and downs. A dip in the market is no reason to abandon a successful strategy, just as a spike in the market would not justify it either. However, when people are within five years of needing that money for living expenses, they should begin to reduce the percentage of their portfolio in aggressive funds, but not abandon them altogether.

- Example: You are age sixty-five, and already retired. You have 50 percent of your retirement investments in aggressive mutual funds, but you do not need income from those funds to pay your living expenses. You have other assets from which you pay your bills. Do you have too much risk in your retirement account? No. If you do not need to spend some of that money within five years, there would be no good reason not to continue pursuing greater returns with that money. If you will not likely need to use that money, those funds will probably be passed on to your heirs through your estate. The time horizon for those investments could be quite long, sufficient at least to weather the shorter-term ups and downs of equity markets, and to increase the size of your financial legacy.

From these two examples you can see that age itself has little to do with how you adjust your portfolio. The important factor is your intended use for the money—your investment strategy.

How Do You Hold Your Assets?

I would like to address one final aspect of investing that is rife with false assumptions, myths, and misunderstandings. My views are contrary to conventional wisdom, so the subject is very important to me. Many people are not using their money as efficiently as they could because they have accepted popular, but misguided, prejudices about three types of portfolio vehicles—the types of accounts in which they hold their assets. The first is tax-deferred retirement accounts, which may be inefficient if they are your only source of retirement investment. The second is variable universal life insurance, and the third is variable annuities. These have been described as the scorned stepsisters of investing, and they're too often overlooked as efficient investment vehicles.

Myth #1: Tax-Deferred Accounts Are the Best Way to Invest for Retirement

This is one of the most pervasive myths in the world of personal finance, and for many people it is one of the more detrimental to their financial health. For many people, tax-deferred accounts are *not* the most efficient way to invest for retirement.

Tax-deferred accounts are all of those that permit a tax deferment on investments from the time the money is earned as income until it is withdrawn. These accounts include 401(k)s, IRAs, SEPs, and Keoghs.

Contributions to a tax-deferred account may be an excellent starting point if you are planning for retirement. But they do present some problems. For one, you are locking up your money for a long time. Generally speaking, you cannot withdraw those funds without a 10 percent penalty until you are 59½. If you are saving to buy a home or if you have consumer debt that needs to be paid off, those may be wiser, shorter-term uses of your money. The other potential drawback to tax-deferred funds lies in the assumption that you are deferring taxes until you are retired, have less income, and may be in a lower tax bracket. That may be a false assumption. Right now, tax rates are at historically low levels, especially for those in higher-income brackets. Are they likely to stay as low as they are now? Not with all our Federal and state governments' current deficits. The quickest fix for deficits is to raise tax rates. You may be deferring taxes until they are higher than they are now.

In "Planning for Retirement" in chapter 1, I lay out the potential hazards, the pluses, and the minuses of tax-deferred accounts in greater detail.

Myth #2: Life Insurance Is Not an Efficient Investment

Life insurance can be much more than an important way to protect your family. It can also be an important part of an efficient *investment* strategy. The primary complaint about life insurance as an investment is that the cost is too high, that investing through life insurance is more expensive than buying mutual funds. While life insurance does have additional cost, cost is not the primary issue when dealing with any investment.

Our focus should be on the value and the investment, instead of cost.

Life insurance has changed dramatically in recent decades, making it an investment vehicle to consider. Of course, my reference is to variable universal life insurance (VUL), a type of permanent life insurance. A VUL is quite different from term insurance, which is a policy you purchase just to cover your life for a certain number of years, but has no investment value.

Permanent life insurance does have higher costs than mutual funds, but those costs may be justified by greater returns, in some cases. Permanent life insurance also offers many tax advantages. Policy payouts to your beneficiaries are often not taxable, unlike IRA investments, which usually are taxable.

Giving Money to Insurance Companies: Term versus Perm

For years the debate has raged: Which is more efficient, buying permanent life insurance, or buying term insurance and investing the cost difference?

A term insurance policy provides a fixed sum for the death benefit for a fixed length of time, usually ten to thirty years. The policy is priced according to the statistical likelihood of the death of the person insured. If you're young and healthy, you can buy term insurance very cheaply, because the odds are against your dying during the term the insurance is in force. If you're old and sick, the cost is very, very high, because it's much more likely that the insurance company will have to pay.

Permanent life insurance (or "perm") is a policy that pays a predetermined death benefit for which you pay a set premium for your life. It covers your life, not for a set period of time, or term, but until you actually die. *Because the permanent policy will almost certainly pay* a death benefit at the time we die, it's naturally more expensive. The payments for that insurance are spread out over your expected life.

The reason I say, "almost certainly" rather than "certainly" is because cashing out of a policy early or dropping a policy is sometimes an option. But the cash value of the policy is available without surrendering the policy.

The higher premium costs are the cause for the debate about whether to buy perm, or settle for term and invest the money saved from lower premiums in other assets. Life insurance companies, mutual fund companies, broker/dealers, and banks all have a stake in whether you buy term or perm; all of them would prefer you buy term insurance. If you buy term and invest the difference, where will you put that money? Of course, you'll avail yourself of the services of these institutions. You'll invest your money with them, probably for a very long time. They get the money, not the insurance companies. (One of the catches to the term versus perm debate, however, is that many people do not actually invest the difference in premiums, but instead, they spend it. But enough people invest it, and that is in Wall Street's interest.)

Why would insurance companies prefer to sell term insurance if they get more money up front by selling perm?

A Pennsylvania State University study had the answer. It concluded that fewer than one term policy in six survives to the end of the term for which it was written, and less than 1 percent of all term insurance policies ever pay a death claim. [3]

As a result, most people who buy term insurance quit paying the premiums before the term ends, and a very low percentage of policies results in claims paid. Since they seldom pay a death claim, one can reasonably assume that insurance companies love to issue term insurance. The money goes only one way, into the insurance companies' coffers.

Life insurance companies are aware of this fact, but most buyers of term life insurance don't consider it. This discrepancy is one big reason why term insurance is a very inefficient use of your money.

Now let's throw in another concept: opportunity cost. Whenever there's a cost in our financial world, we have that cost–and also the cost of not having that money to earn a return. When you add the cost

---

3.   Arthur L. Williams, "Some Empirical Observations on Term Life Insurance: Revisited," *Journal of Insurance Issues and Practices* 7:1 (1984): 52–62.

of lost opportunity to the cost of premiums, term insurance is not nearly as inexpensive as you might think.

Permanent Insurance Changes for the Better

When many of us learned about finances from our parents, the returns you could earn on the money invested in perm insurance, above the cost of the death benefit, were very conservative. On your own, you probably could do better investing the difference in premiums, because the cash value of the life insurance was invested in fixed-interest investments that provided a low return.

The returns on permanent life insurance changed dramatically, however, when variable universal life insurance (VUL) was created in the late 1970s. With a VUL policy, the cash value of life insurance is invested in equity portfolios wrapped inside the life insurance. The internal mutual fund–like accounts are called subaccounts, and they can be compared to retail mutual funds. Insurance subaccounts, in fact, are often managed by the same people who manage retail mutual funds. The performance is likely to be comparable, except for two major differences:

1. The earnings of a retail mutual fund are currently taxable (unless owned inside some type of pretax retirement plan), while earnings in a VUL are not; and

2. The VUL deducts life insurance costs.

The performance of VUL subaccounts may exceed that of retail funds, however, because the managers don't have to be concerned about tax liabilities for shareholders. That potential for improved performance may make up for some of the insurance cost. With access to typical market returns on investment, the VUL offers the potential of significantly better performance than earlier life insurance investments provided. For investors who are middle-aged or younger, and in a moderate tax bracket, it is possible that a VUL policy will *outperform* retail mutual funds. (Note: Both mutual funds and VUL investment subaccounts involve market risk, including fluctuating returns and possible loss of principal. In addition, early withdrawals from, and loans taken against, VULs might involve additional fees and tax penalties, and negatively affect death benefits.)

With the advent of the VUL, you could buy life insurance that would almost certainly pay a benefit someday (unlike term insurance), and has the potential to earn competitive returns. But the advantages don't end there.

Strategic Applications of Permanent Life Insurance

The current tax advantages of life insurance can make it an attractive investment strategy even if you have no desire (or need) for the death benefit. There is a drag on the internal rate of return for the costs unique to life insurance, primarily for the death benefit. However, depending on your age, gender, health, and tax bracket, the tax advantages of life insurance may more than offset the internal costs.

The higher the tax bracket, the greater the advantages. The greatest advantages also will be enjoyed by people who are young and healthy, because the mortality cost of the insurance (the amount you pay for the death benefit) is lower for those who are not likely to die for a long time. Women also enjoy some advantages in the cost of life insurance, because statistically they live longer.

In my experience, permanent life insurance is likely to be advantageous for healthy people up to the age of fifty. After that age, health becomes a critical factor in determining the potential benefits. Even more important is how long one plans to fund the contract or continue paying premiums. I advise at least ten years, preferably longer. The often-overlooked strategic advantage of permanent life insurance in a financial plan is that it can be used as a conduit to other investment strategies. New money goes into perm, which then serves as a "holding tank." We can take distributions from our holding tank for personal use (such as to pay for college or start a new business) or invest in assets not available through the insurance subaccounts (such as a stock opportunity or real estate). We can even take distributions and reinvest them in pretax plans or a Roth IRA, if we should want.

If we have taxable earnings on our new investment, those earnings can then be directed back into the insurance policy and not allowed to compound. Using perm insurance as the conduit to other investments is an effective way to potentially increase benefits and earnings. This is because no new money is wasted by first going into assets that don't produce benefits. Perm insurance does not replace other investments, and is not necessarily "better" than other investments. But it enhances those other investments by making them more efficient.

Let's assume you contribute $5,000 a year to a permanent life insurance policy for ten years, creating an income tax basis of $50,000. However, due to positive investment performance, the contract has grown to $100,000 of equity (cash value). Because the policy has the unique treatment of first-in/first-out taxation, you could withdraw $50,000, and not trigger a tax liability because the withdrawal is treated as a return of the basis (the original amount). However, if you withdrew the entire $100,000, you would receive a 1099 for the $50,000 gain, and that gain would be taxed at ordinary income tax rates. The way to avoid the income tax, if you desire a distribution that exceeds your basis, is to take out a loan from the insurance company, with your policy as collateral.

Most permanent life insurance contracts offer a very low net cost to borrow money against the cash value of your policy. Unlike a withdrawal, a policy loan does not disturb the contract's equity: The company actually lends you money, and the equity in the contract serves as collateral. An amount equal to the loan is set aside and credited with an interest rate generally in a range from 2–4 percent below to the same interest rate you are being charged to borrow. In other words, generally the worst case is a 4 percent net cost, but some contracts even allow for zero-cost loans.

You can see that the beauty of life insurance is that it does provide for the greatest emergency of all, a death, but at its best, it is also a springboard into planning for the rest of your life, and even your legacy if you live to a ripe old age.

Myth #3: Variable Annuities Are Too Expensive

Variable annuities have taken a bad rap. Some financial advisors use them widely, yet many self-appointed media experts on personal finance roundly criticize variable annuities. Why this contradiction?

Think about an annuity as a great replacement for a pension.

Now they're the exception, but until recently, people retired with a pension. A pension paid a fixed amount every month, and continued until you died. Let's say that amount was $4,000 and it began at age sixty-five.

If you were retiring at sixty-five tomorrow, you could well have 401(k) savings that, invested in a conservative bond portfolio, would pay you $4,000 a month by drawing down the principal in addition to interest. But you'd run out of money at age eighty-five. And the actuarial tables say there's a 30 percent chance you'll live that long, or longer. You could make the money last until you turned 100 by taking only $3,000 per month. But then your quality of life would likely be quite different.

That's where we see the strategy of using an annuity. Annuities may help eliminate uncertainty, and produce a guaranteed monthly income that mimics the income from a pension plan. You can use the same 401(k) savings that you put into the bond portfolio to buy an annuity that pays $4,000 per month. And never worry about running out of money. There's no magic to it either. Annuities have the ability to pay longer than individual, self-managed retirement accounts because people who buy annuities and die early end up subsidizing those who die later. That's exactly how a pension plan works, too.

Three more reasons to consider an annuity

1. It may ensure income for as long as you live, and therefore may help reduce the chance you'll be a burden on your children.

2. A "joint-and-survivor" annuity pays until both you and your spouse die, which helps eliminate the worry of income for women, who are likely to outlive their spouses.

3. An annuity can help you know when to retire. It's difficult, if not impossible, to know what kind of lifestyle a lump sum will support in retirement. But when that lump sum is translated into a monthly payment, it's relatively easy to know when you've saved enough to live the way you want.

How to buy an annuity with confidence

Annuities have many good qualities, but being easy to understand isn't necessarily one of them. Your employer probably selected a good choice of 401(k) investment options for you, as well as a good health insurance plan, and maybe even a good term life insurance policy. But companies and 401(k) plans that offer annuity options are few and far between. And for most people, shopping for a complex financial instrument with hundreds of thousands of dollars is frightening.

So look for these three things when considering an annuity:

*   First, differences among policies. The monthly payment per purchase price won't vary. It can't; all annuity issuers are using the same actuarial tables. But many small things, like the ability to make changes after purchase, will be different, and they can be important.

*   Second, a cost-of-living, or inflation, rider. Inflation has been tame for at least a decade, but if it increases, your set monthly payment will be worth less and less as time goes by.

- Third, the rating of the insurance company that issues the annuity. The viability of insurance companies had not been an issue within living memory until the recent Great Recession, when AIG, the largest insurance company in the world, was saved from collapse only by government intervention.

Annuities have changed a lot since the first edition of this book, especially the living benefit options. Today, living benefits typically offer two things that were not offered six years ago. First, a guaranteed rate of return that generally ranges between 5 and 8 percent. These guaranteed rates of return are net of all fees and expenses, but an investor may have to agree to certain provisions in order to achieve the guarantees. For example, one may have to agree not to take any distributions or disbursements from the annuity for a certain period of time in order to achieve the guaranteed rate of return.

Second, variable annuities today offer guaranteed lifetime income. This is different from past years when most of the benefits were a guaranteed return of principal. For example, prior to 2006, if one were to invest $100,000 in a variable annuity, he or she might have received a guarantee that said: "We [annuity company] promise to return at least $100,000 to you regardless of the underlying performance of the investments, regardless of the performance of the stock market, provided that you limit the size of your distributions each year."

Generally, the range of these distributions was 5 to 7 percent. The problem was, if there continued to be a prolonged down market where the underlying investment never made money, and investors could take their 5 to 7 percent out over a fourteen-to twenty-year period of time, and then also recapture their original $100,000 investment, they may have also received a letter from the annuity company saying, in essence: "We promised we'd pay you back at least $100,000, or the amount of your original investment, and now we've done that. The contract is finished; it's over." And the investor thinks to himself, "Well, yeah, but I'm not dead yet, and I still need income."

Today, annuities offer guaranteed lifetime income, not just a return of the original investment. So variable annuities now can provide income not just for the account holders, but also the spouse or primary beneficiary. Today, I could put in $100,000, and when I decide to create an income stream from that, I'm guaranteed that I'll get an income for like, no matter how the underlying investments perform, and no matter how long I live. Furthermore, if I die before my spouse, the income can switch to her, giving her income for her lifetime. Generally, the income stream is contingent upon the investor, and usually on him or her not taking out more than 4–5 percent per year. Therefore, one of the potential disadvantages would be if the investor needed more than 4–5 percent per year. In that case, the investor would be wise to have investments other than a variable annuity. By that I mean they might not do a variable annuity at all, or they might do a variable annuity, but also have other investments where they can take more income. So use caution.

Anyone with a distribution rate exceeding 5 percent per year runs the risk of running out of money before he or she runs out of breath. The attractive thing about the annuity is the income stream of 4–5 percent; it guarantees income for life, and many annuities now also offer the opportunity for increases in income if the underlying investments do well, and the account value goes up. And many firms promise that the income will never go down. For most people, 4–5 percent should be sufficient income to maintain their standard of living anyway, especially if there is the opportunity for increases to keep up with or exceed the rate of inflation.

Here's one reminder that's true of any important financial decision: get good advice. If you're considering an annuity, do it in the context of all the other options available to you. Work with your advisor, and make sure an annuity is the right choice for your specific situation.

Don't Wear Blinders

As you consider investment vehicles, don't wear blinders. Consider all your options. Don't just accept conventional wisdom, and don't listen exclusively to just one "authority" on any of these vehicles—not even me. Test my views, and see if they make sense for you. I know what has worked for me and for my clients, so challenge me as I'm happy to debate my positions with anyone.

Ultimately your investment choices depend on your unique values, goals, and strategy. Explore every possibility. You might find an investment avenue that offers you a better way to achieve your investing goals.

Establish clear goals, and determine the balance of risk and reward you will need to meet them. Understanding and communicating your values helps ensure financial decisions are made based on what is most important to you. If your strategy is clear, you will be able to sift through your many options with a greater understanding of the advantages and disadvantages of various options, such as tax-deferred accounts, variable universal life, and variable annuities. Some may be inappropriate for your plan; others may help accomplish exactly what you want. You'll never know which options are right for you if you don't look at all the possibilities.

Ten Things Investors Worry About Too Much

1. The Federal Reserve. Will it lower interest rates? Is it focusing more on inflation or deflation? As Bill Murray said in Meatballs, "It just doesn't matter."

2. Talking heads. Do yourself a favor. Stop getting your advice from the media. Don't listen to the talking heads. Get an advisor you trust, and listen to your advisor.

3. What your friends are doing. Their situation is different from yours—and when they brag about their great investments, they're probably embellishing. And, by the way, in addition to tuning out your friends, tune out trillionaire investors like Warren Buffett. What he does

would make no sense for most of us. If he's out of the market during a recovery, it's not going to have any impact on his lifestyle. But for those of us who rely on certain investment returns, being out of the market if there's a recovery could definitely impact our lifestyle. You have to focus on your goals, your objectives, your time horizon, your risk tolerance, the rate of return you need, and what you're going to use the money for. Focus on yourself.

4. The investment's cost. Cost is only an issue in the absence of value. What features or benefits are provided by the extra cost? Are they worth it?

5. The calendar. Summer rally? January effect? October swoon? Again, who knows?
   It's time—not timing.

6. Every single investment they own. Some will be up; some will be down. That's normal. Don't worry about it. If you do, ask yourself, "Do I really trust my advisor to put me into these investments?" Look at the big picture, and don't worry daily about each individual investment.

7. Cost basis. Gains or losses are what they are. So what. If you made a lot of money, you pay some tax; your net-net is still attractive and still desirable.

8. Stocks you sold. After you sell a stock and it continues to do well, do you kick yourself? Don't. If your investment strategy is sound, and the sale was part of your strategy, forget about it. Even if you made the mistake of investing emotionally, and were reacting to temporary market news or conditions, move on. Focus on your strategy—and promise yourself that your future actions will be based on strategy, not emotion.

9. Stocks you never bought. We've all done it. Every day some stocks soar and others tumble. Get over it. Mathematicians will tell you that, over time, any random series of numbers will regress to the mean. So if you flip a coin ten times, you could get "heads" on nine flips. If you called heads every time, you'd have a 90 percent success

rate. Phenomenal! But if you continue for another 10,000 flips, you'll be very close to 50 percent. The corollary in the investment world is that over time, your performance will be roughly equal to broader market returns. And that's a good thing given what we know about historical returns on investments. Of course, investment performance is not purely random. How can you improve your likelihood of success? Not with stock picking, but with asset allocation.

10. Short-term performance. Nothing—positive or negative— can be determined in the short term. Anything related to the stock market has got to be measured in long blocks of time, five years or more.

Investing: A Concise Summary

1. Develop an investment strategy tailored to your life, your values, and your goals.

2. Start now. Time is your greatest ally.

3. Allocate investments into a variety of asset classes according to your investment time horizon and risk tolerance. Negative correlation is desirable. If you hope to earn a return that beats the effects of inflation, your asset allocation should include some investment in stocks. Returns on stocks, measured by broad market averages, have been remarkably consistent over the past seventy years.

4. Continuously manage your investments and rebalance your portfolio at least once a year to maintain your desired asset allocation.

5. Do not rely solely on any single type of retirement portfolio vehicle. Tax-deferred retirement plans have a place in your plan, but not to the exclusion of other possibilities such as variable universal life insurance, variable annuities, or Roth IRAs. Do your homework, and understand any product before investing.

6. Do not try to time the market. Let time work to your advantage. History demonstrates that it will.

7. Rely on your core values and your strategy, not your emotions. By following a strategic path, you will not be sidetracked by fear or greed.

Paying Taxes

Taxes can be a complex and often-overlooked element of a financial plan. Yet tax planning is critical to long-term financial success. Obviously, your goal is to pay as little tax as possible. But just as you never want to invest without considering tax implications, you never want to invest for *only* tax reasons. Tax reduction is one part of the potential total return that you must analyze. (At the end of this chapter, the Your Money Matrix section explains how to consider tax implications strategically when you invest.)

Three File Cabinets

When exploring how investments may be treated for tax purposes, it's useful to think of individual filing cabinets:

- Cabinet 1 is for taxable investments: Earnings on these investments are fully taxed in the year earned. These types of investments are generally non-retirement accounts.

- Cabinet 2 is for tax-deferred investments: Taxes on these investments are not paid when earned, but are deferred until withdrawn, such as with 401(k)s and traditional IRAs.

- Cabinet 3 is for tax-advantaged investments. This category includes investments that do not reduce taxes now, but the earnings and distributions are income tax–free over time. Investments in this category include Roth IRAs, Municipal Bonds, and Life Insurance.

Taxable Investments

The first file cabinet would contain all of your taxable investments or savings. We won't distinguish here between investments that produce ordinary income and investments that produce capital gains. Taxable investments include money-market accounts, CDs, mutual funds, stocks and bonds, and everything else where income or loss is fully taxed when earned. All of these types of investments give you almost immediate access to your money when you need it.

Try to have enough money in liquid accounts to cover living expenses for three to six months. Liquid assets are assets that can be converted into cash (liquidated) quickly at any time. A checking account is very liquid; a Stradivarius violin or a 1952 Mickey Mantle baseball card is not. The violin and the card may be worth far more than your checking account, but you couldn't just sell them on the street corner. You would have to find a qualified buyer, which could take some time, and the buyer would have to meet your price. If you were forced to unload your violin or Mantle card quickly, you might have to sell at a substantial loss, or at least at a price well below the current market value.

Occasionally you will hear someone talk about having a "liquidity" problem. That could mean the person is worth billions, but those billions are all tied up in investments that can't be liquidated easily. It could also mean that a person is flat broke, and is putting a dire situation in the best light.

You can avoid the worst liquidity problems by maintaining some investments in the first file cabinet: taxable investments.

TaxDeferred Investments

The second file cabinet holds your tax-deferred investments. This category would include any nonqualified tax-deferred annuity, individual retirement account (IRA), simplified employee pension, 401(k), 403(b), Keogh, 457, or any other pretax retirement plan. In these investments, the amount of the contribution is deducted from your income for tax purposes in the year in which you make the contribution. Most investors put the lion's share of their investment dollars into this file cabinet. Overfunding these types of investments can actually be inefficient and counterproductive.

Tax-Advantaged Investments

The third file cabinet is for tax-advantaged investments. An ideal financial plan has dollars in all three file cabinets. Unfortunately, for most investors, the tax-deferred file cabinet is overflowing, and they do not even have a third file cabinet. Tax-advantaged investments would include those that may be tax-free or tax-deductible or that give the investor a tax credit. The essential difference between this file cabinet and the second one is that tax-advantaged investments aren't just taxed at a later time; all or part of the earnings from a tax-advantaged investment might not be taxed at all.

Obviously, all things being equal, tax-free is preferable to taxable or tax-deferred.

Relative to pretax retirement plans, most people put too high a percentage of their resources in the second file cabinet, and ignore the third. Investments that are potentially tax-free include municipal bonds, some life insurance, and Roth IRAs. In many cases, your earnings on those investments are not subject to income taxes.

Don't wait for the target to stop moving, however, because it won't. Tax policy always has been and always will be tinkered with by presidents and Congress. It's impossible to predict what will happen with tax rates and tax policies, so create the best tax plan to account for present tax law, and make adjustments to your plan as changes occur. The most important thing is to get the advice of professionals well before tax time comes.

Taxes: A Concise Summary

Three lessons can be drawn from any close examination of tax policy and its impact on individuals:

1. The current tax system allows tax-reduction strategies. Many people who should be taking advantage of them don't even consider them. They are overlooked, in part, owing to an overreliance on tax-deferred retirement plans. Most people, with more careful and detailed tax planning as part of an integrated financial plan, could reduce their tax burden now and in the future, including taxes on their estates.

2. The current tax system is extremely complex, and keeping up to date requires a lot of what could be otherwise productive time for CPAs and other financial professionals, not to mention our elected representatives. Wouldn't the world be a better place if that brilliance could be applied elsewhere?

3. Individuals who try to do their own financial planning cannot possibly keep up with the complexity and the changes in this industry. This illustrates a constant theme in this book and everything I have ever written, every lecture I have ever given, every radio show I have ever done: People should not try to do this themselves. Seek the help and guidance of a qualified and trustworthy financial professional.

Application: Your Money Matrix

In the introduction to this chapter, I wrote about your financial "pie," and how you slice it. All the ways you can use money are interrelated. A good example of that is Your Money Matrix, a tool we developed at our firm to help guide investment considerations as well as the impact of taxes. Now that you have a basic understanding of primary investment considerations and the tax cabinets into which investments may be put, let's examine Your Money Matrix.

For each row, we add a column that indicates the estimated annual cash flow from all the assets in that row.

Your Money Matrix provides basic guidelines for approaching asset allocation in the broadest terms with the tax implications of investments clearly in mind. Obviously, your age and personal values and goals play a central role in the mixture of investments you would choose.

Your Money Matrix encourages you to consider both your financial future, and the efficient use of money, in broader terms than perhaps you do now. Most people have too high a percentage of their assets in the taxable and tax-deferred columns, leaving the tax-advantaged column empty.

Here's a good exercise. Plug your assets into each of the rows and columns to see if your investments truly meet your goals and time horizon. Are all of your assets crammed into one box? Is it realistic for you to spread those assets more evenly among the boxes?

Your Money Matrix™

Time Horizon	Taxable	Tax-Deferred	Tax-Advantaged	Estimated Annual Cash Flow
Short-term income (0-5 years)	Money market; Bank deposits; CDs; Treasury bills, notes; Corporate bonds	IRA (conservative); Corporate retirement plan (conservative); Fixed annuities	Roth IRA (conservative); Municipal bonds (short term); Fixed % life insurance	
Medium-term growth and income (6-14 years)	Money market; Bank deposits; CDs; Stocks; Real estate; Investment trusts; Treasury bills; Intermediate Corporate bonds	IRA (moderate); Corporate retirement plan (moderate); Variable annuities (balanced, moderate)	Roth IRA (balance, moderate); Municipal bonds; Variable life (balanced)	
Long-term growth (15+ years)	Stocks; Long-term CDs; Real estate; Investment trusts; Long-term corporate bonds; Treasury bonds	IRA (aggressive); Corporate retirement plan (aggressive); Variable annuity (aggressive)	Roth IRA (aggressive); Tax credit investments; Tax-deductible investments; Variable life (aggressive); Municipal bonds (long-term)	
Total Investments	$	$	$	$

Your individual objectives will make this a very personal tool to use in planning your financial future. Few people complete this matrix the same way because their lives and aspirations are not identical. Some place a priority on retirement investing; others add investing to pay college tuition; still others focus primarily on creating an inheritance for their families. The Your Money Matrix exercise will help you focus more clearly on your goals, and see the actions you may need to take to accomplish those goals. It is a very useful step—once you understand the fundamentals of money and your personal approach to money.

Sharing Your Wealth

For many people, giving money to a faith community, charity, community or arts organization, an educational institution, or victims of natural disasters is a primary motivation for financial planning. Even for many of my clients who don't have large net worths, giving some money to others is very important, either during their lives or upon their deaths.

My family and I believe strongly in the importance of making charitable donations. Many clients have asked my advice, and then made generous contributions to their favorite nonprofit organizations. They have been delighted to make those gifts—and to discover that they may also receive significant economic benefits from their generosity.

Giving can be a rewarding part of your financial strategy, and you can do it in ways that benefit both you and your favorite organizations or causes.

Why Give?

Over the years, I have encountered nearly every reason imaginable for making contributions to charitable organizations. The most common, however, are the following:

- Compassion for those in need;

- Religious and spiritual commitment;

- Desire to perpetuate one's beliefs, values, and ideals;

- Support for the arts, sciences, and education; and

- A desire to share "good fortune" with others.

The tax laws of the United States encourage these gifts, and in many cases, grant them tax deductions. If individual citizens voluntarily help meet our country's needs, their contributions reduce the government's responsibility. Many would also argue that private support of charitable activities is more efficient than public support.

Due to the tax treatment of charitable contributions, individuals might not only realize immediate tax benefits, but also *advantages* in terms of after-tax cash flow, as well as the size of the estate they may pass on to their heirs.

Gifts to charity during one's lifetime or at death, if structured properly, will reduce the estate tax liability. An additional benefit of lifetime gifts is that an income-tax deduction is available within certain percentage limitations.

A Farm, a Church, and a Family

How can giving money away provide economic benefits beyond the tax deduction? Let's consider the case of Howard and Betty, who were in their early sixties when they came to me.

They had owned and operated a family farm for forty years, but they were preparing to sell their farm for $1.2 million to a real estate developer. Their cost (basis) in the property was about $200,000, so they would have a gain of $1 million. That gain would be taxed as a long-term capital gain at a Federal rate of 15 percent, for a liability of $150,000. This was a big tax liability, but they would still net $1.05 million after taxes. Assuming a fairly conservative hypothetical investment rate of return of 8 percent on a portfolio, the proceeds from the farm sale would generate $84,000 in income per year without invading the principal.

During an introductory meeting with Howard and Betty, I discovered two important things. First, they were very spiritual people who gave a lot to their church, and wanted to do even more for it. Second, even though they felt blessed to have a $1,000,000 gain on their land, net of tax, they were unhappy about having to pay $150,000 in taxes, but they felt there was nothing they could do about it.

I advised Howard and Betty to create a Charitable Remainder Trust (CRT), and fund the trust with the property. Then the CRT would sell the land to the developer. Because the asset would be sold through the CRT, there would be no capital gains tax liability for Howard and Betty. The CRT would provide them with an income stream of $96,000 per year (8% x $1.2 million) instead of $84,000. They would also receive a tax deduction now for the future gift to their church, because when they died, the remainder of the trust would go to the church. The gift they could make to their church was the primary motivating factor for Howard and Betty to pursue this strategy, but it also gave them an extra $12,000 of income each year that they could not have any other way.

The one flaw that Betty and Howard saw in the plan was that they would be disinheriting their children. Although they wanted to give a lot to their church, they also wanted to leave something for their children. We solved the problem by using the tax deduction over five years, and fully paying for a $1 million last-survivor or second-to-die life insurance policy, so their children would have $1 million income tax–free to split after Betty and Howard passed away.

The result of this strategy was to:

- Make a profound gift to their church;

- Increase Howard and Betty's annual income;

- Generate a significant tax deduction they could spread over five years; and

- Protect their children's inheritance by using the tax savings created by the deduction to purchase life insurance at essentially no out-of-pocket cost.

Howard and Betty felt very good about their gift, which certainly did a lot of good for their church, and they also increased their income, as well as the money they left to their children.

You may find, as Howard and Betty did, that a gift to your favorite charity, if structured properly, actually increases your after-tax cash flow during your lifetime. Moreover, your charitable contributions enable you to decide how your money is used, rather than letting the government decide for you.

Your charitable gift may provide economic benefits to both you and your heirs. Although that may not be your primary motivation for giving, it can be a very attractive fringe benefit—one that is readily available, and one that could be used by many more people if they planned carefully.

Giving Sooner or Later

Tax laws pertaining to charitable contributions can be very complex, and allow for many types of gifts.

- **Cash gifts.** The simplest form of donation in terms of tax treatment is an outright gift of cash or other valuable assets. Within certain limitations, such gifts generate income tax deductions at the time the gift is made, and also reduce the estate tax liability.

- **Wills.** Individuals who might depend on income from their assets to meet their needs often designate a portion of their estate to go to a charity upon their death. Such a bequest, if properly structured, will reduce the estate tax liability.

- **Split-interest gifts.** These gifts are a method of widely used charitable giving that is much more complicated, and can take many forms. In the interest of simplicity, I will provide a very general description. Please consult professionals to determine the various forms these gifts might take.

I covered different strategies for sharing your wealth in detail in chapter 4, so I won't repeat them here, but I'll remind you that these giving strategies are not do-it-yourself undertakings. You will need assistance from professionals to do it properly so that both you, and the organization you are contributing to, obtain the maximum benefit from your gift. The last thing you want to happen is that not you, your heirs, or your favorite charitable organizations receive the full benefit of your generosity. The IRS has strict rules on what is permissible if you are doing anything more complicated than making a straight cash gift.

Many charitable, religious, and educational organizations will provide considerable assistance to you in handling the legal and accounting aspects of making a gift to them. It makes sense to discuss your desires and plans with the organization as early as possible to make the most of their assistance and expertise.

What those organizations may not be able to provide, however, is advice on where your gift fits with your values, and in your overall financial plan. Will your gift create unanticipated hardship for you at some point? Is your gift actually much smaller than you would like to give and could comfortably afford to give if your money were working more efficiently? These questions can be answered only in the context of a complete financial plan that takes into account your needs, your values, and your investment strategy.

It may seem like a lot of hassle to go through just to give your money away, but it would be inefficient for you and your favorite charity *not* to take advantage of the tax breaks available by doing it the IRS's way.

Don't sell yourself short by planning your retirement based on some arbitrary percentage of your income. "Needs planning" is a good start for someone who has given no thought to retirement savings. It's a way to convince people that they should save something, but it's not good for people who want to do better than get by. Don't settle for mediocrity in your investment planning. Try to excel. It's fine to set a floor for what you will need, but then aim higher—and *plan* to get there. Become a "wants" planner, instead of a "needs" planner. Only when you determine what you want from life, can you determine the role money will play in helping you achieve your dreams.

The Great Unknown

Will you live to be 100 or will you die earlier, perhaps much earlier? The greatest fear of many people, especially as they approach their golden years, is that they will run out of money before they run out of breath.

Without a crystal ball, we can't say for certain when that will be. We do know, however, that we are living longer than ever before. For people born in 1900, it was statistically unlikely that they would live until age fifty. Today, just over a century later, your life expectancy is between seventy-five and eighty years.

A comprehensive financial plan helps you prepare for the certainty of uncertainty. It acknowledges and prepares for death (premature death that is before statistical life expectancy) by using life insurance efficiently. But you should also acknowledge and prepare for the possibility that you will live beyond age 100. You should plan for both scenarios, since you can't possibly plan to spend your last dollar on your last day on earth.

Three Planning Phases

In the face of that great unknown, financial planning requires you to consider three phases of your financial life: *accumulation, distribution,* and *legacy or transfer of wealth.* Nearly everyone focuses on the first of those phases, accumulation, and ignores the others until they are near or in retirement. In effect, a simple focus on accumulation of assets is not much better than not planning at all. It's a bit like tucking your money in your pocket and jumping in your car to start your vacation, without any idea where you are going.

1. *Accumulation* concentrates on gathering and growing assets. You can accumulate wealth many ways: saving what you earn, being the beneficiary of life insurance, inheriting wealth, investing in securities that grow in value, building up a business to increase its value, and earning interest on a savings account (although this will not likely outpace inflation). All financial service organizations and their representatives—stockbrokers, insurance agents, financial planners, CPAs, or other types of advisors—are interested in helping you in the accumulation phase of planning.

   We all want to see our portfolios grow without any losses. Most people tend to think of financial planning as a process of accumulation, coupled with tax deferment through pretax plans such as 401(k)s or pension funds. This simplistic approach focuses mostly on the accumulation phase.

2. *Distribution* focuses on how you spend your assets when the time comes that you no longer live off your wages, or you choose to live off the value of accumulated assets. Good distribution strategies include a) an estimated cost of living adjusted for inflation and lifestyle, b) the order in which you spend your assets, tax-deferred investments, and legal tax avoidance tactics, and c) certain types of insurance products. This phase of financial planning takes much training and continuing education on the part of the financial advisor, and focused effort by both the advisor and the client. Although many stockbrokers, insurance agents, and bankers are able to provide some of these products, it is usually CPAs and financial planners who assist in creating distribution strategies that best suit individual needs.

3. *Legacy or transfer* addresses what you ultimately wish to do with your assets. Some of these strategies include family limited partnerships, charitable and other foundations, riskbased products (life and disability

insurance), tax-reduction strategies, formal estate planning, and trusts. Usually lawyers, CPAs, banks, insurance agents, CFPs, and highly experienced financial advisors provide these services.

Planning is the only way to make sense of the five things you can do with money.
If you don't plan, you will likely spend more, save less, invest less, and do nothing to reduce your taxes.

CHAPTER 6

Why Hiring a Professional is to Your Advantage

At the beginning of this book we talked about how basing your financial journey on your personal values will lead you to make better decisions about your money. Now, to help you successfully complete that financial journey, I'm also advising you to engage a terrific financial advisor with whom you can work as one. This chapter is about how to find that person.

The relationship you have with your financial advisor is as intimate as with any other professional who serves you. It's just that instead of being about your health, or your teeth, or your legal issues, it's about your money.

And I do mean intimate. A financial advisor cannot serve you well unless he or she gets to really know you. Your financial plan should revolve around your most dearly held goals and aspirations. This requires a level of knowledge and insights into your personality and life that likely you'd reveal only to a handful of others. If some personal connection is not present, perhaps you hired the wrong person to help you with your financial planning.

This section may seem self-serving, but I believe in the services I provide and the value I deliver. I've shared some guidelines important to your financial life, but this book can't cover every subject or every contingency. For you to be in the best possible financial health, you need the expert advice of a qualified and competent financial advisor.

This section gives you some of the information you will need to find the right person to advise you and play an integral role in helping you achieve your dreams.

Finally, it is worth noting that the most financially successful people, including Warren Buffet, Bill Gates, and Oprah, engage financial advisors. They don't do it themselves.

Who Can Help? The Focus of Financial Professionals

The efforts of most professionals tend to have a narrow focus. Find the one that best meets your needs.

Stockbrokers. Most stockbrokers help primarily with the accumulation phase. They usually earn commissions on trades, and focus on the success of your portfolio. Most have a shorter-term approach to investing, concentrating on the best possible returns at any given time, rather than a longer-term view that helps you get to where you want to be.

CPAs. Certified public accountants are primarily tax specialists, not investment specialists. Although many try to help their clients reduce tax liability through investments, and many even broker specific investments, their focus is usually on the tax implications of an investment, and not where the investment fits in an overall financial strategy.

Private bankers. Banks tend to focus on trusts, so they offer legacy/transfer services, but usually not broad-based planning.

Insurance agents. Insurance agents focus on risk or the legacy/transfer phase of planning. They are often also well versed in certain types of insurance-related tax-deferral or tax-avoidance products. Most do not, however, offer well-rounded financial strategies. Many insurance companies have now established financial planning services that are available not through the agent, but through the parent company, thus they tend to offer only products created by the parent company.

Attorneys. They work primarily on estate planning, a legacy/transfer niche. While estate planning is useful for many people (I strongly advise it), in the absence of an integrated financial plan, it can play only a limited role in an efficient financial strategy.

Financial advisors. Okay, I'm biased, but this I believe:

- Only professional financial advisors who are not tied to a specific company's products or range of investments can offer effective assistance on all three phases of a financial plan—accumulation, distribution, and legacy/transfer.

- Financial advisors can take your financial plan beyond accumulation strategies to address distribution and legacy/transfer issues as part of a comprehensive plan.

- Independent companies that have specialists in all of the planning phases offer the most comprehensive service.

Because it's not easy to choose someone to guide your financial plan, I have devoted several pages in this chapter to help you select a financial advisor. Can you create your own financial plan? If you have the time and aptitude, you probably can do much of the work yourself, with the exception of tax planning. The tax code is so complex that few people have the stomach or the stamina to master it on their own. I know I don't.

This book provided a foundation on some basic principles, but no book can guide you through all the variations and considerations that are appropriate to your circumstances, your life, and your dreams.

The problem with creating your own plan is that, as in most fields, you probably don't know what you don't know.

No More Excuses

People have a lot of excuses for not planning. Whether you intend to hire someone to help you or decide to go it alone, start your financial plan now. It is very difficult to make up for lost time, whether years or decades, in making your money work efficiently to help you achieve the future you want for yourself and those you love.

Most important, write down your questions, and then reflect on and make a list of your values and your goals. That's how I begin with my clients: I ask them to write down their core values and goals in life, not just their financial goals, and to be as precise as they can be. If you are not clear about your goals, it is impossible to achieve them. If you don't have dreams or aspirations, if you think only about everyday life, you'll remain stuck in the rut of the mundane.

Yes, of course, you have to take time to smell the roses, to play with your kids, but even that will be more enjoyable for you if you believe you are focused clearly on the future you desire, and what you have identified as most important to you.

The best way to predict the future is to *create* the future. The journey of a thousand miles begins with a single step. Begin now. Once you get started, once you set a plan in motion, momentum takes over. Think of it as a buffet line. The line may be long and slow, but at least you're moving. You're going to get your meal faster than if you wait for the line to get shorter.

The Future of Financial Services

The world of financial services has changed dramatically in the past decade, and change will continue. Consolidation of the big financial service providers also is likely to continue. Those service companies will focus on speed and technological efficiency, often at the expense of personto-person service. Their focus will remain, simply because of the size required for efficiency in that arena, on the execution of financial transactions, whether writing a check or buying a stock, for people who already know what they want. But those companies are ill suited to providing personal advice to clients.

The nature of companies that have traditionally provided narrow advice in the investment arena will also change. I stand by my prediction that in the nottoo-distant future, stockbrokers will disappear. Their focus is too often on specific investments without regard to strategy, portfolio, or long-term financial planning goals. Stockbrokers who are bullish on a particular investment recommend it to all the clients in their database, whether or not it is appropriate.

Moreover, with technological advances and the public's increasing familiarity with those technologies, primarily the Internet, investors are able to do their own research and make their own trades far more cheaply than they can through a broker. If brokers serve primarily as simply the executors of trades, they offer little value for their charges.

How brokers are compensated is also inherently flawed, as it promotes trading activity, rather than success. If your broker sells some of your ABC stock, he is compensated based on the transaction. If he uses that money to buy XYZ stock, he is compensated again. How either stock performs does not affect his compensation. Most brokers are paid when, and only when, they execute trades. That is a poor platform from which to help their clients meet their long-term goals.

People who rely on stockbrokers are placing greater importance on picking stocks than on their overall financial strategy, which does not give you the best chance of success financially. Successful financial planning requires much more than deciding which stocks to buy. To increase the efficiency of your money, you probably don't need stock-picking advice as much as you need expertise on the U.S. tax code or advice on a wider variety of investments that offer advantages you may not find with traditional equity investments. Those are areas in which most brokerages do not provide much assistance to any but the wealthiest clients.

The accounting industry has already gone through an earth-shaking change, with the largest firms consolidating and one, Arthur Andersen, disappearing in the wake of charges of complicity in the Enron debacle. The behemoths of the industry will continue to serve primarily corporate clients, with smaller firms targeting smaller businesses and individuals.

By the process of elimination, the future of personalized, comprehensive financial services is me—and many others like me. I'm able to draw on the expertise of accountants, lawyers, and investment managers, as well as experts in insurance, to provide my clients with comprehensive financial planning and management services, all under one roof. I spend time with clients; I get to know you, and then tailor a financial plan to your unique needs.

The Value of a Financial Advisor

The reasons for choosing someone to help formulate and execute a financial plan to achieve a dream will vary from one person to another as much as the dreams themselves. Whether you lack the time, the expertise, or the stomach for worry to create your own financial plan, a professional should be able to provide valuable assistance.

Choosing a financial advisor is intensely personal. You will reveal information to your advisor that you would reveal to very few others, and you will give that person an extraordinary responsibility for helping you achieve your dream. Beyond the empirical or factual evidence of a financial advisor's ability to meet your needs, you have to trust and place your confidence in that person. All facts being equal, trust your intuition. If you actually like the person and enjoy your interaction with him or her, the process of achieving your dream will be much more enjoyable—and never forget that enjoying life is one of the ultimate purposes of money.

Whether you use a financial advisor or create your own plan without expert assistance, always remember that you are in control of your money. Someone else may sweat about the details, and take the worry of dayto-day money management off your shoulders, but you are the CEO of your money. When you hear or read advice from any source about how to create wealth, think about it carefully, and whether it applies to you and your situation.

A lot of conventional wisdom does not apply to you, whether you hear it from your friends, your relatives, or your financial advisor.

Adding Value

A good financial advisor can add value in many ways:

- **Helping clients identify their core values.** By understanding values, the advisor will know the "complete you," and then he/she is poised to help you make better financial decisions.

- **Creating additional investable capital.** Many consumers have inefficient strategies in place. A good planner can suggest strategies that can free up more money to invest without detracting from one's lifestyle.

- **Being objective.** Many otherwise intelligent people can have a hard time being objective about their own personal finances.

- **Identifying goals.** A good planner can help clarify a vision of one's future.

- **Saving time.** Many people are so busy with the day-to-day demands of work and family that they want to delegate responsibility for their money.

- **Worrying about your money for you.** Most people realize they don't have the desire, time, or aptitude to manage their own money efficiently. Therefore, they worry about it. I tell clients that it's my job to worry for them, and if they are still worrying after I'm on board, then maybe they should hire someone else.

Why do many of my clients hire my services? Because I'm smarter than they are? Neither they nor I believe that. They hire me for what I know, even though they are capable of learning what I know. It's just not how they choose to spend their time.

In my office, on the street, at parties, and on my radio show, I'm asked one question more than any other: *How do I determine the best way to take distributions from my retirement plan?* The frequency this question is asked underscores the need to work with a professional advisor. If you think the purpose of financial planning is only to accumulate assets, you are seeing only half the picture.

Good financial planning not only helps you accumulate assets efficiently, but also helps you distribute them efficiently.

Many of my clients, now in their fifties, are just beginning to think about distributions. It is already too late to avail themselves of some of the most effective accumulation and distribution strategies. If you're in your fifties or sixties, you can still make smart decisions to enhance your life and your wealth, but if you're in your twenties or thirties, you have so many more available investment tools and vehicles. Financial advisors serve a very useful purpose if they do nothing more than get younger people to begin considering options and strategies. Begin planning your distribution strategy as you are planning your accumulation strategy.

The goal of enhancing your wealth is also to enhance your life, however you choose to do it. A whole-life planning approach, a plan for your accumulation years as well as your distribution years, will help you do that. That's why you need the services of a good financial advisor.

When asked this distribution question, unless I know your full financial profile and your goals in life, I can't answer it very effectively. That's because, like most people, you are not "average"—and taking advice aimed at "average" investors can be risky.

You Can Do It Yourself (Maybe)

If you devote the time and energy to it, you may be able to create your own financial plan—with one very important exception: You probably will *not* be able to integrate effective tax strategies into that plan, even if you do consider your investments' tax liabilities.

Taxes are the big complication, and likely the largest single cost in your life.

- Determine how you can reduce taxes as much as possible.

- Pay what you must, but pay no more.

- Use tax strategies that present an enormous opportunity to use your money more efficiently.

Even if you do create your own plan, be sure to hire the services of a qualified professional who can examine your tax consequences, and perhaps recommend alternative strategies that will reduce your taxes.

Do you think that you don't have enough assets to qualify for tax-reduction strategies? You may be surprised at how little you need to invest to avail yourself of these opportunities, especially if you don't concentrate simply on reducing taxes *this* year. Too many people rely too heavily on tax-deferred plans, in a sometimes-shortsighted effort to reduce taxes *now*. They get a tax deferment this year, but it may not help at all in years to come.

Tax deferment in pretax plans may be nothing more than seeking instant gratification at a greater cost in the long term. In that sense, it's not a lot different from spending your money on something you want, instead of investing it with the intention of getting a bigger reward at a later time. Just because you reduce your taxes this year, don't think that you are avoiding them in the future—you might not be.

Plan for the longer term. Assess the tax consequences of your plan several years out or into retirement. That's what real planning does: It examines all the variables of your finances well into the future. Professional financial advisors should be better at this task than you are.

How You Will Pay

Two options are available. You pay an advisor a fee for services, or you pay commission on the sale of products, or perhaps both. The advantage of working with an advisor who charges fees instead of earning commissions on products is that you avoid conflicts of interest because he or she is not trying to sell you anything. However, because fees are the sole profit center, they may be high. Moreover, a fee-only advisor has no motivation to inspire you to implement a plan, so it may collect dust. If a financial advisor earns commissions on the sale of products, look for someone who is independent, instead of an employee of a financial products company.

Find an advisor who can offer solutions from a variety of resources so that you get the best strategy to meet your core values and goals—and not what a parent company pushes your advisor to sell.

A financial advisor should be able to provide (and explain) the value that justifies the cost of services. Financial authors and magazines that are critical of various planning and investment strategies–for reasons of cost–frequently overlook the benefits purchased by that cost.

In hiring a financial advisor, as in determining the execution of your investment strategy, focus on value instead of just cost.

How to Choose a Financial Advisor

By now I hope you are convinced that using a financial advisor is a good idea. Now, how do you go about choosing one who will deliver the value that justifies the cost? Start with a personal referral from someone whose opinion you value. Even then, you should still interview the candidate. Ultimately, your decision will be instinctive rather than intellectual.

Over the years, hundreds of people looking for someone to help them manage their finances have interviewed me. In the process, I've learned what is useful to them, and I've developed a keen sense of what questions elicit information that I would want if I were in their shoes.

My list is boiled down to ten questions. The first nine are useful, but the last, which is frequently asked, often reveals nothing that will really help you.

1. What professional designations does the advisor have? The designation, or lack of a designation, does not necessarily indicate the planner's competence. On the one hand, some people in the financial industry try to present themselves as financial planners in an attempt to enhance their credibility, even though they are not qualified. On the other hand, pursuit of a professional designation can demonstrate a commitment to the profession. And don't discount experience in the industry—it counts for a lot as well. The designations I deem relevant are:

    •   Certified Financial Planner (CFP®)

    •   Chartered Financial Analyst (CFA)

    •   Chartered Financial Consultant (ChFC®)

    •   Certified Public Accountant (CPA)

2. How many years has the advisor been working in the industry, and how did he or she get started? The financial service industry has a high attrition rate. Many firms actually recruit representatives with the idea that the newly hired representative will establish accounts with friends and family and then ultimately fail and leave the industry, but the new clients will stay because they don't know where else to go.

3. Has the planner ever been fined or suspended by a regulatory agency? Consumer complaints are to be expected with an advisor who has practiced a long time with a lot of clients. But to be fined or suspended indicates wrongdoing. Find out if there might be a reasonable explanation.

4. How does he or she get paid? Financial advisors earn their compensation in two ways:

    1. Fees
        A. Time
        B. Management
        C. Plan preparation

    2. Commissions on sale of investment products

    It is also widely believed that if an advisor receives commissions, it will cost the investor more. That simply is not true. When you plan a vacation, do you call all the hotels in and around your ultimate destination? Do you personally check out all the times and costs of flights, and then book your flight? How do you arrange your car rental? Many people make one call to a travel agent who will do all of those things. Furthermore, the cost is the same as (or even less than) if they arranged the trip themselves. Acquiring financial products is similar to planning a vacation with a travel agent. You can acquire products directly from the entity distributing the product or through an agent—the financial planner—and the fees and costs are often the same.

3. Is the advisor captive to a larger corporation? (Does he or she sell proprietary products?) Many so-called financial planners are really product salespeople. If they're aligned with a specific company, they may have a vested interest in selling that company's products. Advice: Find an independent financial advisor, with a fiduciary responsibility to you, and not to a parent company.

4. How many clients does the advisor have? If the advisor has very few clients, you might wonder how proficient he or she is. If he or she has too many clients, you may wonder about the level of service you will receive. Find out what you can expect from your advisor. Then you will be able to measure whether or not he or she delivers.

5. How many support people does the advisor have? And what is their expertise? Ask a prospective planner how big his or her staff is today, and how big it was last year and the year before. It's important to know whether the organization is growing, and what is the ratio of support staff to advisors. The number of people in support roles will tell you something about the level of service given. To give you a benchmark for evaluating staff support, I believe that four to six people for every financial advisor is a good support ratio.

6. How does the advisor address issues on which he or she is not an expert? No one, including me, can know all there is to know about personal finance. But I have formal working relationships with people whose job it is to follow and track developments in specific fields, such as taxes and accounting. In my experience, having those specialists available is important; their advice is invaluable to me, and it allows me to deliver the right value to my clients. If the advisors you interview do not have formal working relationships with such experts, find out how those issues will be resolved, and what it will cost you if outside assistance is required.

7. What is the average net worth of the advisor's clients or the range of clients he or she serves? Financial advisors

may have a specialty or a focus that doesn't suit you. An advisor who serves primarily clients who have net worths in the millions of dollars might not have the knowledge or the interest in working with those who have less money to invest. You may get lost in the shuffle of big-buck deals. On the other hand, if advisors work primarily with people who have less money to invest, they may not know the intricacies of more advanced planning and investing techniques, such as trusts and tax-advantaged investments. Such an advisor may suit your needs now, but will he or she still be able to help you as your net worth grows?

Most important, find someone who listens to and understands what *you* want to accomplish. Less effective financial advisors are as likely to fall victim to myths and to old habits as does the average consumer. In the day-today crush of work, they may rely on off-theshelf, one-size-fits-all investment strategies that are little better than the myths embraced by your Uncle Bob.

8. Will the advisor provide references? Of course. Every advisor will probably be able to provide names of clients who would give him or her a favorable recommendation. That's why I say don't bother asking for references. The advisor will give you the names of only those who have a good opinion of the services they receive—and you don't know whether those people are astute investors. Are they qualified to evaluate the services they receive? You can only guess.

Getting Ready to Create a Plan

Choosing a financial advisor isn't the end of your responsibility. Regardless of whom you choose, I say again: you are still the CEO of your money, and it's up to you to ensure that you are gaining full value from your advisor's services. A good advisor can only make recommendations, not tell you what to do. So you still need to supervise your advisor and your financial plan. On the next few pages, I provide a framework for your decision-making.

Also, recognizing that some of you will still insist on trying to do a financial plan by yourself, the advice here will help you do it as well as possible, assuming that you enjoy all the disciplines involved in creating and implementing a good financial plan.

If you intend to create your own plan, however, you have to be brutally honest with yourself from the beginning. Many people have the best intentions when they sit down to create a plan, and they might even do a pretty good job. But that's not where the biggest problems arise.

The real problems arise in the continuous management of that plan (bear in mind that these issues refer only to investment management, which is the tip of the iceberg in comprehensive financial planning):

- Preventing style drift in your portfolio or the funds in which you've invested;

- Rebalancing regularly to maintain the ideal asset allocation;

- Changing your allocation as your needs change;

- Keeping abreast of tax changes that could give you a window of opportunity to alter your plan to your advantage.

After a while, many investors get careless and begin to let their plans slide. Their portfolio no longer represents the asset allocation they selected. Or worse, their asset allocation accurately reflects their situation or needs of ten years ago, even though their lives have changed dramatically.

Think hard, not just about the knowledge you'll need to acquire or the time it will take to create a plan, but also about the commitment of time and energy to manage it effectively.

1) Dream a Little Dream: Know Where You Want to Go

Slow down. Before you even begin to gather all the information that you'll need to create an investment strategy, sit down (with your spouse or partner, if you have one) and let your mind roam.

What do you really want from life? If you could do anything you want, what would you do? Don't put financial restrictions on yourself now. Dream. Stretch a little. Once you have that dream defined, once you know roughly where you want to go, you can begin to determine what role a financial plan can play in helping you live that dream.

2) Gather All Your Financial Information: Know Where You Are

The second step is to gather all the information you'll need. You can't plan unless you know where you are. In my practice, I ask my clients to obtain the documents and provide the information noted below.

Documents

Get together the following financial and legal documents:

- Federal and state income tax returns for at least two years

- Most recent pay stubs

- Statements from all investment accounts

- Documentation of all company retirement, investment, and insurance plans, including benefits, beneficiary designations, and costs

- All personal life, health, disability, long-term care, and Medicare supplement policies and statements

- Estate planning documents such as wills, trusts, powers of attorney, and living wills; if you don't have a will, this is an excellent time to prepare one

- Documentation related to involvement in all business or personal matters that could affect your personal financial situation, such as buy/sell agreements, non-compete agreements, consulting agreements, and deferred compensation plans

- Social Security and pension benefit estimates

Assets and Liabilities

Make a list of all of your assets and liabilities. If you are planning with a spouse, be sure to note which assets are in whose name or whether they are jointly held.

When you list your liabilities, be sure to include complete information on your loans for your primary residence, second home, cars, boats, and other recreational vehicles. This information should include original balance, current balance, monthly payment, length of loan, and the interest rate, as well as whether those obligations are personal or jointly held.

For any fixed-interest investments, list the current value and the interest rate. For equity investments, list the average growth rate for each stock or mutual fund. List your taxable, tax-deferred, and tax-free investments separately. Be sure to include any insurance policies, including disability insurance, companysponsored plans, and annuities.

For each asset that you own, also include the amount you add to that investment each month or each year.

Income and Expenses

You're not finished identifying where you are yet, because you still have to determine all of your income and expenses.

Don't calculate only your present income; try to project expected annual increases as a percentage of your present income. You want to have as clear a picture of your future income as possible. Include wages and salary, bonuses, self-employment income, interests or dividends on investments, Social Security, rental property income, pensions, alimony, and any loans you have made to others.

Make a realistic effort to determine what your living expenses are for a year. It may be easiest to break it down monthly, and then add those up to get your yearly expenses. This by itself is a good exercise in financial discipline, because most people don't think they're spending as much as they are. When determining your expenses, be sure to add any estimated major expenses you will incur in the future, such as college education costs for your children.

You know the different kinds of professionals who can give you financial advice. And you know the reasons to choose an independent financial advisor, the services independent financial advisors can perform, and how they charge for their services. You know the questions to ask and how to get ready to create a plan with your new financial advisor.

There's nothing left to do but begin. Follow your personal values, keep this book handy as a reference, and you'll do fine. You may even have a great time doing it.

CHAPTER 7

The Last Word: Love

At the beginning of this book I posed a question: After the collapse on Wall Street, and its effects on Main Street, and the new economy that's rising unsurely from the wreckage, what's still solid in the financial landscape? And I answered it: Your values and the people you love. They're the basis of your financial plan, and of all the other financial decisions you make. They always have been, and they always will be.

So with all the details and advice on the preceding pages still swimming in your head, don't forget my answer. Keep your focus on the critical constant in this book: the people and values that are important to you. The rewards you get in life from loving the people and living the values will far surpass and outlive the rewards of any money you accumulate, distribute, or leave as a legacy.

The priority in your life should never be the money. Those you love can thrive with less money if they have your love; they cannot thrive if they get your money without your love. Money is only one tool among many that can be used to manifest your love for them, to provide for them, to enrich their lives.

You may have a lot of money, or you may have little. It doesn't matter. What matters is whether the money is used well or poorly to improve the lives of those you love.

The rest is the tactics in these ten simple guidelines that summarize what I've written:

1. Dream

2. Make a plan

3. Eliminate debt

4. Live within your means

5. Invest systematically

6. Allocate assets

7. Ensure investment efficiency

8. Reduce taxes

9. Adjust your plan as your life changes

10. Enjoy life

Remember that without love in your heart, for one or for many, money in the bank has little value.

One More Thing

In this book, I discussed and sometimes compared different investment products. Each addresses certain investor needs, and each has distinct risks and rewards. Some of those differences are so marked that regulators require that financial professionals spell them out whenever we discuss these products, even in a book that does not purport to give advice about products and investment strategies for any specific individual.

With that said, here are facts about some of the investments I discuss in this book and about investments in general:

- Equity investments involve market risk, including fluctuating returns and possible loss of principal.

- Unlike equities, bonds offer a fixed interest rate and return of principal if held to maturity.

- High-yield bonds typically involve more risk of issuer default than investment-grade bonds.

- Government securities are backed by the full faith and credit of the United States and are considered to be among the safest investments.

- International investments involve special risks, including economic and political uncertainty and currency fluctuation.

- Small-capitalization stocks tend to experience greater volatility than large-capitalization stocks.

- Mutual funds and variable-rate contract investment subaccounts involve fluctuating returns and values so that an investor's shares, when redeemed, may be worth more or less than their original cost. In addition, early withdrawals from, and loans taken against, variable-rate contracts may involve additional fees, tax penalties, and/or negative effects on death benefits.

- Money market mutual funds are neither insured nor guaranteed by the U.S. government and there can be no assurance that they will maintain a stable net asset value of $1.00.

- Real estate and other sectoral investments may be subject to sectoral or regional economic downturns.

- Direct participation programs are generally illiquid and involve special risks. They may not be suitable for all investors.

- Unlike securities, CDs and other bank deposits offer a fixed interest rate and are FDIC-insured to $100,000.

- The Dow Jones Industrial Average, the Standard & Poors (S&P) 500, the Russell 5000, and other indexes are unmanaged and are provided for benchmark reference purposes only. Investors cannot invest directly in indexes.

- Periodic investment plans do not assure a profit, nor do they protect against losses in a declining market. Dollar cost averaging involves continuous investment in securities regardless of the fluctuating price of such securities. Investors should carefully consider their financial ability to continue their investments during periods of low price levels.

- Past performance does not guarantee future results. The reason is simple: The markets will never be exactly the same again.

Throughout this book I used many examples to illustrate financial concepts. These examples often use hypothetical rates of return for different kinds of investments. In all cases, these rates of return are for illustration only and do not represent any specific investment.

Did you get all of that? Curiously enough, authors who do not hold the licenses and have the training and background I have can write whatever they please. They can and often do make outrageous claims and dispense horrible advice without anyone challenging them. It's as if they ran red lights and caused accidents, but the police had to let them go because they didn't have a driver's license.

ABOUT THE AUTHOR

Bruce Helmer is an award-winning financial advisor and co-founder of Wealth Enhancement Group, a financial advisory firm based in the Twin Cities area in Minnesota. A financial services industry veteran, he has been in the industry since 1983. Bruce has been host of the *Your Money* radio show since January 1997. The format of the show is educational; financial topics are introduced, and then followed by unscreened listener calls to which Bruce responds to on-air. *Your Money* is one of the most-listened-to financial education shows and it reaches more than 50,000 listeners each week with sound financial advice.

In addition to working with clients, writing, and hosting his radio show, Bruce speaks frequently on leadership, motivation, and personal finance topics.

Bruce's guiding philosophy is simple: He wants your money to work as hard for you as you work for your money.

If you're interested in booking Bruce for a speaking event, or to order additional copies of *Real Wealth*, visit **BruceHelmer.com**.